The Seven Pillars of Church Revitalization and Renewal

Tom Cheyney

Biblical Foundations for Church Revitalization

ISBN:0990781666
ISBN-13:9780990781660

DEDICATION

To Cheryl, my beloved!

My best friend, life companion, and the one who challenges me every day to be the best I can for my Lord. You mean the world to me. There are so many things I truly admire about you as a person, as my best friend and as my wife. Your smile lights up my soul. As a church revitalizer's wife, you have been courageous to go even when the path seemed unclear and yet the hand of God was certain. You have given much and sacrificed more so others might see Jesus.

To all of those Church Revitalizers serving in local churches asking God to do great things and revive their church once more: the course is not easy, but the need is great and our Master longs to see the church restored for future generations.

"For God has not given us a spirit of fearfulness, but one of power, love, and sound judgment"

2 Timothy 1:7 HCSB

To God be the glory forever and ever.

The Seven Pillars of Church Revitalization
Table of Contents

Acknowledgements

I am blessed to serve each day the Greater Orlando Baptist Association (GOBA). This is a growing network of churches that is changing the way we have done associational work across Southern Baptist congregations. No longer bound by geography, GOBA has raised the bar by working with churches, networks, and partners to plant healthy churches, revitalize those churches in need of renewal, and develop leaders equipped for the ministry through the GOAL Leadership Development Training. The *Renovate National Church Revitalization Conference* is one of many new things that have impacted Christianity cross-denominationally, and is spearheaded by the wonderful pastors and laity who have partnered with us for the work of the Lord. To you, may I say thank you.

To the many committed Church Revitalization Practioners who join with me annually to make the Renovate National Church Revitalization Conference the largest conference focused on helping declining churches, I thank you. Your gifts and your passion for hurting churches make my heart leap over such godly compassion. To those just beginning the journey, seek God's best and become your best daily so you become a vessel fully developed for the work of a church revitalizer.

To my friends and fellow church revitalizers Bob Whitesel, Terry Rials, Michael Atherton, Rodney Harrison, Gerald Brown, Walter Jackson, Ron Smith, Larry Wynn, Chris Irving, Rob Hurgen, and Paul Smith: you have taught me so much about leading change and I truly am grateful. Thanks Bob for partnering with me to host the Renovate National Church Revitalization Conference annually.

Lastly to my Strategic Director of the Renovate Conference, Mark Weible, I say thank you for knowing and showing daily how to do team. You have lightened my load many times so I could find an afternoon or evening to finish some of this manuscript. You quietly influence, Mark, thousands of church revitalizers monthly by the work you do to advance the cause of church revitalization and renewal. The best is yet to come.

Tom Cheyney, Founder & Directional Leader
Renovate National Church Revitalization Conference

Introduction
The Seven Pillars of Church Revitalization and Renewal

Our Lord loves the local New Testament Church and it is His desire to see it grow! The need for Church Revitalization has never been greater in North America. An estimated 340,000 Protestant churches in America have an average weekly attendance of less than one hundred.[1] Research data tells us that in the United States more than 80% of the churches have plateaued or are declining.[2] Each and every week we are currently seeing somewhere between fifty and seventy-five local churches close their doors, not to be opened again. Pastors leading churches today admit that there are daily frustrations that distract them from doing the real work of ministry. Focus on the Family estimates that 80 percent of pastors and 84 percent of spouses are discouraged or are dealing with depression.[3] Badgering people creating badgering issues drain pastors of the must needed strength to deal with the real issues of growing a church and

---

[1] Hartford Institute for Religious Research (hirr.hartsem.edu/research)

[2] Research Source: Stats listed online at: http://www.newchurchinitiatives.org/morechurches/index.htm (accessed 2/23/2006).

[3] James Dobson, Focus on the Family, "The Titanic. The Church. What They Have in Common" (August 1998). www2.focusonthefamily.com/docstudy/newletters/A000000803.cfm.

reaching the lost for the Lord Jesus. The smaller the church the more these pressures affect the local church leadership. The Pew Foundation released a startling report in 2008 called the Religious Landscape Survey, where they revealed that there was a large group of individuals that switch churches or drop out.[4] In that same year, the American Religious Identification Survey discovered:

"The percentage of people who call themselves in some way Christian has dropped more than 11% in a generation. The faithful have scattered out of their traditional bases: The Bible Belt is less Baptist. The Rust Belt is less Catholic. And everywhere, more people are exploring spiritual frontiers – or falling off the faith map completely. So many Americans claim no religion at all (15%, up from 8% in 1990), that this category now outranks every other major U.S. religious group except Catholics and Baptists."[5] Everything that must be done in the area of church revitalization cannot be accomplished in a few hours on the Lord's Day!

The hard reality in North America is that most churches and most if not all denominations are in a state of decline. The membership within these

---

[4] Cathy Lynn Grossman, *USA Today*, "Survey: American Freely change, or Drop, Their Religions" (5/30/2008). *www.usatoday.com/news/relgion/2008-02-25-survey_N.htm.*

[5] Cathy Lynn Grossman, *USA Today*, "Most Religious Groups in USA Have Lost Ground, Survey Finds" (3/17/09). www.usatoday.com/news/religion/2009-03-09-american-religion-ARIS_N.htm.

churches and denominations are plateauing and what used to pass for involvement and activity within churches is deteriorating. While all of this is happening, the rank and file of the church appears powerless to assemble the strength that is needed to get the churches growing again. Kevin Ezell, President of the North American Mission Board of the Southern Baptist Convention declares, "We must keep our denominations focused on the ministry of rebirth and redemption, not on the business of enforcing rules and rituals."[6] In 1990, editor for the *Wall Street Journal* Wade Clark Roof published an editorial article entitled, "The Episcopalian Goes the Way of the Dodo," where he argued the decline of mainline denominationalism and its effect on Christianity.[7] With the turn of the twenty-first century sustained growth within our churches has become an intermittent exception while decline seems to be more of the pronouncement. The mainline denominations to which Roof referred, are still in the midst of severe decline and serious deterioration. Stuck in the status quo, new wine cannot be poured into the same old wine skins of outdated mindsets. A new sense of urgency is required for lasting change. Change is required and the church in need of revitalization and renewal cannot escape change. Will we allow the church of America to become mirrors of the churches all across Europe that

---

[6] David S. Dockery, Ray Van Neste, and Jerry Tidwell, *Southern Baptists, Evangelicals and the Future of Denominationalism*, (Nashville: B&H Publishing Group, 2011), i.

[7] Wade Clark Roof, "The Episcopalian Goes the Way of the Dodo," *Wall Street Journal*, July 20, 1990.

find themselves empty urns holding the obvious? We must not.

The most recent research data, released in January of 2012 by the *Leavell Center for Evangelism and Church Health*, has said that within my own Southern Baptist Convention we are at a critical juncture regarding church plateau and decline. The most recent series of studies have been conducted by Bill Day, who is the Associate Director of the *Leavell Center for Evangelism and Church Health*, and who serves the New Orleans Baptist Theological Seminary as the Gurney Professor of Evangelism and Church Health. His sequential studies chronicled church health and growth in 2003, 2007, and 2010. In January of 2012, Bill Day reports that currently there are less than seven percent (6.8) of our SBC churches that are healthy growing churches. That means 3,087 of our 45,727 SBC churches are healthy. Even the number of SBC churches is in decline and we need to address the needs for church revitalization immediately.

Charles Stone has examined the challenges to ministry that pastors face and lead to their frustration. These ministry killers are:

1. Head-in-the-sand mentality
2. Misdirected emotional investment
3. Unhealthy responses to ministry killers
4. An attitude that "God and I can handle this"
5. Lonely hurting spouses[8]

---

[8] Charles Stone, *Ministry Killers and How to Defeat Them*. (Bloomington, MN: Bethany House Publishers, 2010) pg. 11.

The Seven Churches of Asia Minor[9]

In August of 1997, I created the chart you will see throughout this book dealing with the seven pillars of church revitalization and renewal. I have been asked many times if I were to do it again would these specific seven still remain as the chief ingredients for renewal? The answer is that while I am sometimes attracted to the thought of adding one or two more, the simple response is that these are all found within scripture together as the Lord addressed the seven churches of Asia Minor. Adding additional ideas just is not supported by the scripture upon which I have based all of my renewal thinking.

These chapters speak of local church revitalization with perhaps a clearer voice than any other passages within the New Testament. The seven Asian churches were real, historical first century churches, yet the messages given to them are relevant to the church of today worldwide. The letters are more in the nature of messages than letters. Each message to an individual church was apparently intended for the other six churches as well.[10] Each of the seven messages originates with an individual depiction of Jesus taken from the vision of Christ given in the first chapter of Revelation. Kendell Easley says:

> Each one is a permanent reminder of the special relationship the risen Lord had with a

---

[9] C.f. Revelation 2:1-3:22

[10] Alan F. Johnson, vol. 12, *The Expositor's Bible Commentary* (Grand Rapids, MI: Zondervan Publishing House, 1986), 431.

congregation he loved. When Paul, Peter, John, James, and Jude wrote their epistles, they generally followed the customary five-point formula of the first century: (1) author and recipient names; (2) formal greeting; (3) prayer; (4) main message; and (5) formal conclusion. Jesus created a letter-writing formula found nowhere else: (1) a *characteristic* of the sender; (2) a *compliment* to the recipients; (3) a *criticism* against the recipients; (4) a *command* to the recipients; and (5) a *commitment* to all who overcome.[11]

Robert Jamieson and others in *A Commentary, Critical and Explanatory, on the Old and New Testaments* state the following regarding the addresses to the seven churches:

Each address has a threat or a promise, and most of the addresses have both. Their order seems to be ecclesiastical, civil, and geographical: Ephesus first, as being the Asiatic metropolis (termed "the light of Asia," and "first city of Asia"), the nearest to Patmos, where John received the epistle to the seven churches, and also as being that Church with which John was especially connected; then the churches on the west coast of Asia; then those in the interior. Smyrna and Philadelphia alone receive unmixed praise. Sardis and Laodicea receive almost solely censure. In Ephesus,

[11] Kendell H. Easley, vol. 12, "Revelation", *Holman New Testament Commentary*; Holman Reference (Nashville, TN: Broadman & Holman Publishers, 1998), 33-36.

Pergamos, and Thyatira, there are some things to praise, others to condemn, the latter element preponderating in one case (Ephesus), the former in the two others (Pergamos and Thyatira). Thus the main characteristics of the different states of different churches, in all times and places, are portrayed, and they are suitably encouraged or warned.[12]

The conclusion of all the letters is composed of a final exhortation to heed what has been said and a promise of salvation. This concluding exhortation is identical in all seven letters, though in the first three letters the formula precedes the promise, while in the last four letters it follows the promise. *"The one having ears, let him hear what the Spirit says to the churches"* is revealing as G.K. Beale remarks *"The one having ears, let him hear"* is based on virtually the same wording in the Synoptic Gospels, which itself alludes to Isa. 6:9–10.[13] He further explains, "In the Gospels this exhortation is a formulaic exhortation to heed the message of the symbolic parables. In its paradigmatic New Testament use[14] it has the dual function of signifying that symbolic revelation will be received by the elect but rejected by unbelievers. Therefore, the exhortation assumes a mixed audience, of which only a part will respond positively. The formula also shows that

---

[12] Jamieson, et al., Revelation 1:20–2:7.

[13] G. K. Beale, *The Book of Revelation: A Commentary on the Greek Text* (Grand Rapids, MI: W.B. Eerdmans; Paternoster Press, 1999), 228-36.

[14] C.f. Matthew 13:9–17; Mark 4:9, 23 and Luke 8:8.

Christ's words are none other than the words of the
Spirit and that Christ dwells among the churches
through the Spirit."[15] It should be noticed that all the
cities to which these seven messages are delivered were
situated outside the boundaries of the Holy Land and
that the Christian Church in each community was
certainly composed of Gentile converts. Three of these
churches are living as the Bride of Christ and four of
these are yielding to the influences of the world. In
arguing the biblical rationale for church revitalization
within the Seven Churches of Asia Minor, we see a
vivid picture of the Church with all of her graces and
all of her failings. We see the Church when it is strong
and when it is weak. These churches present the
Church in times of joy and times of sorrow. The Asia
Minor examples given through John show us a church,
which is tempted and falls while displaying a church
which returns to the ways of the Lord. These seven
churches are the primary bases of church revitalization
and renewal and have been broken down into the
seven pillars (Tables 1 & 2) of church revitalization.[16]

Working in the area of Church Revitalization will
lead you to eventually consider the Seven Pillars of
Church Revitalization. As a Church Revitalizer, you
will not be working in all of these areas at the same

[15] G. K. Beale, *The Book of Revelation: A Commentary on the
Greek Text* (Grand Rapids, MI: W.B. Eerdmans; Paternoster Press,
1999), 228-36.

[16] For more information regarding the *Seven Pillars of Church
Revitalization* by Tom Cheyney go to: RenovateConference.org or
search *ITunes* for the *Church Revitalization & Renewal* podcast
posted weekly by the Greater Orlando Baptist Association.

time but you will eventually find yourself working in most of them at one time or another. Take a moment to reflect upon the following illustrations of the Seven Pillars as we discuss these areas of renewal and revitalization.

Table 1

The Seven Pillars of Church Revitalization Pillar	Seven Churches of Asia Minor (Biblical Passages) Biblical Foundations for Church	Seven Churches of Asia Minor (Specific Pattern) Specific Church Pattern
Revitalization & Realignment	Revelation 2:1-7	Ephesus: where the world came to the Careless
Re-visioning	Revelation 2:8-11	Smyrna: Church which receives the Crown of Life
Refocusing	Revelation 2:12-17	Pergamum: the Church Wedded to the World
Renewing	Revelation 2:18-29	Thyatira: the Corrupted Unrepentant Small Community
Restarting	Revelation 3:1-6	Sardis: the Has-Been Dying Church
Reinvention	Revelation 3:7-13	Philadelphia: the Holding-On Faithfully Serving Church
Restoration	Revelation 3:14-22	Laodicea: the self-sufficient Apostate Church

Table 2.

CHAPTER ONE
The Revitalization and Realignment of the Church

Perhaps the easiest pillar to address, some observers of church revitalization and renewal argue that the era of small churches is over and that the future belongs to the arising mega churches across North America. Granted, "mega" is an amazing phenomenon of the past thirty years which seems to have arisen with the concept of the massive campus church. But to ignore the 340,000 plus churches in North America that average less than 100 weekly in church attendance would be ill-advised! Those who serve and those who attend these churches are an enormously significant network of Christian influence. Even the mega church finds itself struggling to avoid plateau and decline.

Realignment means to put back into proper order or alignment, such as a readjustment, restructuring, shake-up, reshuffling, reorganization, rationalization, or rearrangement; to cause to form new arrangements or to have a new orientation; reorganize.[17]

---

[17] *American Heritage® Dictionary of the English Language, Fifth Edition.* S.v. "realignment." Retrieved July 13 2016 from http://www.thefreedictionary.com/realignment

A church in need of revitalization and realignment is characterized as one where there is the plateauing or declining after a phase of recent or initial expansion. This phase is followed by the beginning of a high turn-over of lay leaders, then a shorter duration of stay of fully assimilated people within the work. The church morale and momentum level typically then drops, and the church coasts for a brief time and then drops again, only to see the cycle of decline repeated again and again. The result is that the church hits a new low each time! This new normal is the first sign of a church in need. Successful churches are aware of their specific strengths and talents. Unsuccessful churches needing to embrace realignment have no clue what their specific strengths are and subsequently flounder around, never making a significant impact on the community they serve. Successful churches choose multiple ministries that align to those talents. Unsuccessful churches wallow around trying one new ministry after another, never finding achievement in ministry and continuing to wear their membership out. Successful churches find cultural environments that value these talents. Unsuccessful churches fail to connect in significant ways with the community because they never take the time to learn the new culture or seek ways to embrace community for Jesus's sake.

The Ephesus Church is certainly a church where the world and all of its trappings came to the careless church.[18] The Lord Jesus knows the

---

[18] C.f. Revelation 2:1-7.

weaknesses of his churches as well as their strengths. Within this short message to the Church in Ephesus, He gives them both well-deserved compliments and well-defined challenges as to its shortcomings. The Ephesus Church had a history of great leaders with the Apostle Paul, Timothy, and later the Apostle John all serving as leaders within this church. Yet here is a church that has become proud and careless in its witness. They had forgotten that servants of the Lord as shepherds are in fact mere gifts given by the Lord God himself.[19] A fundamental truth within church revitalization understands that church health, growth, and success are not guaranteed forever and that some churches need to be warned to worship Jesus and not the leader leading from the pulpit. Here is a church that had many good and great things happening, yet it became lax with its witness. It served others, was busy doing acts of kindness, labored exhaustively, endured various trials patiently, and sacrificed tremendously for the cause of Christ, yet even in the midst of its greatness it became careless. It forgot its "*first love*." Even churches that appear on the outside as almost perfect, on the inside can become unfocused and drift into reckless habits that hinder the gospel's advancement. With all of the successes and victories that the church in Ephesus enjoyed, it was in danger of watching its light be extinguished.

They were watchful to maintain the purity of

---

[19] C.f. Ephesians 4:11.

the teaching by the apostles; sadly, the Ephesian Christians were not attentive in witnessing to the same faith in the outside world. This is what is meant when Christ reproves them for having left their *"first love."* The point is not primarily that they had lost their love for one another, as argued by most commentators.[20] Nor is the point simply that they had lost their love for Christ universally. The idea is that they no longer communicated their previous ardent love for Jesus Christ by witnessing to Him throughout their world.[21] G. K. Beale in his commentary *The Book of Revelation* declares that this is why "Christ chooses to introduce himself as he does in verse one. His statement that he *"walks in the midst of the seven golden lampstands"* is intended to remind the introverted readers that their primary role in relation to their Lord should be that of a light of witness to the outside world."[22] In losing their *"first love,"* it was equivalent to becoming an un-zealous witness for Christ Jesus. A church that loses its *"first love,"* is a church in danger like the Ephesus church of becoming a careless church and in need of revitalization. When we lose our diligence in our gospel witness we become careless, our spiritual gifts are depressed and therefore the chastisement by the Father is warranted.

---

[20] E.g., Moffatt's translation, *"you have given up loving one another as you did at first."*

[21] Beale, 228-36.

[22] Ibid.

With any church realignment the challenge is in the details of implementation. There are risks, challenges and issues to identify, address and manage. Realignment can be as small as rearranging a few key ministries, staff positions or a major re-positioning of the entire ministry strategy eliminating outdated ministries or non-producing staff members. It could mean realigning of the entire church to be more ready to embrace the new changes within its community. Letting go of perpetuating the status quo is often the first initial portion of any realignment effort.

Here are some initial ingredients to the implementation of your realignment efforts: See the end clearly and develop action plans in order to reach the desired end result. List the benefits and risks the church must accept. Remind the congregation of the things that will not change. Be specific about the change that will occur. Communicate early and often. Develop a timeline for your realignment implementation. Have an implementation plan. Bring key leaders aboard early and receive their buy-in. Manage the expectations and reduce the negative talk by keeping all informed. List who will be responsible for what will be done, when it will be done, and how it is going to be carried out. Develop critical implementation milestones. Consider creating an implementation team or working group. Train on the front end, in the middle of the effort, and in the final days to assure you remain focused on the large goal of revitalizing the church. Replace non-productive leaders that are hurting the future of the church revitalization effort. Get the dead wood either off the bus or into a new place of service. Empower your church staff and listen to their advice. Develop trust with as many church members as possible. Work towards overcoming any resistance to change.

CHAPTER TWO
The Refocusing of the Church

Refocusing is the second pillar, and it helps churches that are growing but still need to set new challenges and look for new opportunities to expand their gospel witness into their target area. Questions related to your church's biblical purpose and why you exist as a congregation must be addressed. Looking at how God has showed up in the past is a good way to get the church unstuck by addressing where it has been, how God has worked and what He holds in store for its future. Refocusing is all about rediscovering your specific church's calling. Addressing the church's focus and vision, and then leading them to discover God's new direction is just the beginning of helping a congregation to refocus on the Lord's new calling plan for their church. Many a pastor today have never been taught how to grow a church; they feel quite stuck and in need of someone to come alongside them and challenge them to refocus both themselves as a pastor as well as their congregation.

The Church at Pergamum was a body of individuals that was wedded to the world and all of its evilness.[23] Conceding to the devil is very dangerous for the Christian church. The church at Pergamum was not only one that was wedded to the world and made concession after concession; it was a church that compromised its core beliefs in order to get along with

---

[23] C.f. Revelation 2:12-17.

the world. It was the leading religious center of Asia
Minor. John commends the church in Pergamum for
continuing their commitment to him, even though
some there had perverted moral truths.[24] Very similar
to its nearby neighbor Smyrna, only fifty miles south, it
too confronted emperor worship. Believers were
persecuted harshly for refusing to worship the
emperor. The believers in Pergamum were viewed as
disloyal and lacked being patriots of the community by
those who were not Christians. Pergamum had the
first temple dedicated to Caesar and promoted the
imperial cult. In Revelation 2:13, it is given the name
"Satan's seat" as a reference to how bad it was for true
believers to live. It was even worse for Christians there
than for those living in Smyrna. A believer and
"faithful witness" named Antipas was killed for refusing
to go the ways of the world as so many were doing. In
spite of intense suffering by the Christian church in
Pergamum those believers were not without fault in
God's eyes.

Christ standing over the church as a threatening
judge because of the church's sin is the thought
pervading the entire epistle to Pergamum.[25] *"The throne
of Satan"* in Pergamum is a way of referring to that city
as a center of Roman government and pagan religion
in the Asia Minor region. It was the first city in Asia
Minor to build a temple to a Roman ruler (Augustus)
and the capital of the whole area for the cult of the

---

[24] Easley, 38-40.

[25] Beale, 245-56.

emperor. The city proudly referred to itself as the "temple warden" of a temple dedicated to Caesar worship. Life in such a political and religious center put all the more pressure on the Christian church to pay public homage to Caesar as a deity, refusal of which meant high treason to the state.[26] Within the church at Pergamum there existed a group of individuals which began compromising toward the ways of the world and Christ says that He has something against them in that He hated their everyday practices and doctrines. In such an atmosphere as Pergamum it would be difficult for believers to maintain the high standard of their faith without running into the political and cultic conflict that was all around them. In this passage, God calls them teachers of the *"doctrine of Balaam"* (2:14) and said that they *"lorded it over"* others and led them away from God's teachings and practices. Balaam was a prophet who prostituted his individual gifts so he could earn money from King Balak which had hired him to curse the Israelites.[27] The Lord halted Balaam from cursing Israel and turned his curses into blessings. The sad and revealing portion of this Old Testament story is that by following Balaam's advice as Balak sought to make friends with the people of Israel, he led many to worship pagan gods and feast at their pagan altars. The visual compromise and example from the Old

---

[26]Ibid.

[27] C.f. Numbers 22 – 25.

Testament served as an illustration of the church at Pergamum becoming wedded to worldly ways as it made compromises and concessions with the secular political world which it lived.

The key truth in relation to church revitalization and renewal within this passage is that when a congregation or an individual compromise with the world in order to avoid or alleviate suffering, pain, or failure they are committing spiritual adultery and being unfaithful to the Lord. Such a compromising, permissive spirit of idolatrous living is to be condemned. Churches cannot and must not harbor compromisers of the gospel. The image of the *"sword of my mouth"* is a warning to the church for not disciplining those compromisers, which have entered the church fellowship.

When church members argue wrongly that the church needs to have a closer alliance with the pagan culture it is never correct. Pressure to compromise was becoming an influence facing those within the Pergamum church. Although we have little specific information, the false teachers in Pergamum must have been teaching a subtle distortion: violation of conscience is quite all right, especially if there is not a clear Christian teaching at stake.[28] The false teachers in Pergamum must have been teaching grievous moral error: violation of the marriage bond is quite all right if done in the name of religion. Kendell H. Easley

---

[28] Easley, 38-40.

suggests "they were arguing some variation of the following: Christ came to abolish the Law; part of the Law was the command about adultery; therefore, those in Christ are free to engage in whatever sexual relations they find "meaningful." Such teachings would appeal to those from pagan religious backgrounds in which promiscuous sex was accepted as a routine part of life."[29]

Repentance was called for and the only remedy for one's sin. "Repent, therefore." Not only the Nicolaitanes, but the whole Church of Pergamos is called on to repent of not having hated the Nicolaitane teaching and practice.[30] Christ responds vehemently, to their compromise and declares that he will have none of it. The believers in Pergamum must repent, recognizing and forsaking their sins.

Here are a dozen refocusing questions to help you re-dream where you and your church must travel. The initial preparation period must look at a church's Biblical calling and purpose in ministry. The questions are:

1. Why do we exist as a Church?
2. Where have we been?
3. How has God worked in our past?

---

[29] Easley, 38-40.

[30] Jamieson, et al., Revelation 2: 12–17.

4. Who has God shaped us to be?
5. What are our core values?
6. Where are we going?
7. Whom has God called us to reach?
8. What is God calling us to accomplish in the future?
9. How will we get there?
10. How should our ministries grow together?
11. How will we carry out our calling?
12. What is our plan for the next chapter of our ministry?

In order to begin to Re-focus a church you must:

R – be **Ready** to embrace new things. Honor the past but move towards your long-term goals to grow.

E – Examine the present realities of your ministries and programs for the good and the bad. If they are not working, focus must be placed on what will.

F – Forward looking as you frame what you will do to reach your community for Christ. If your membership is unwilling to reach its community perhaps the best thing you could do is to give it to an organization, which will seek to restart a church renewal effort utilizing those facilities.

O – Open to new people and programs. When visitors stop returning to your church you can be assured that they are not the problem but you and your membership is. Seek new ways to draw the community back into your church.

C – Centered on the Gospel. The Gospel is not only the entryway into the Christian life, but it is the pathway of the Christian life. It is the outrageous news of what has been done for us by God in Jesus. Specifically, the Gospel is the startling news that what God demands from us, He provides for us.

U – Understand that your methodology will look different than mine! Refocusing churches will need to work on various systems within the church and recalibrate them. I might choose evangelism first while you might choose governance. I might place a huge priority on visitors and potential prospects while you might spend more time on anchoring the present constituents before reaching into the community sector. Personally, I would probably place a huge emphasis on growing younger and reaching young families, which could bolster the children's ministry. You might select the youth group because in your area that is a larger demographic you could reach.

S – develop the **Skill Sets** that are deemed necessary in church revitalization. Recently while teaching a doctorial seminar on Church Revitalization at a seminary in Kansas City, we considered some of the vital skills (a baker's dozen) that were deemed necessary for pastors or church leaders to acquire when working in church revitalization or renewal. Here they are:

Prayer Warrior: Far too many leaders today are ignoring prayer in their personal lives as well as leading the church to be a people of prayer. Becoming a prayer warrior, as well as drawing other prayer warriors around you, is ever so vital to church revitalization! Stop ignoring the reality of original sin in the church, as only prayer can confront this reality through the guidance of the Holy Spirit.

A Spiritual Individual & Leader: It is easy for a shoot-from-the-hip type leader to lead a new church plant or even go to another church and pull out his "bag of tricks" all over again. It is entirely something new for a revitalization leader to stay with a ministry and mission that is hard and see it through to its best days. A principle worth noting is that it is not this aggressive, shoot-from-the-hip type of leader that typically makes a strong leader for church revitalization!

Enabler/Encourager: In the area of church revitalization and renewal, it is extremely important to realize that the goal is not to win the battles or wars, but to enable a congregation to move as united as possible into its own new future! The enabler has that wonderful gift and skill set of uniting the church and getting it working together again.

Initiator: The initiator is one who can demonstrate that it is a new day for the church and that victory can be achieved. One of the strengths of this individual leader is the ability to bring people close together through the creation of uniting nudge activities. Nudges are those little things that eventually build upon one another to create big things for the local revitalizing church. Here are some things that I - and others as well - have used to begin the gentle nudge of their church into renewal and revitalization: facility improvement (a little paint, rearranging the mess, cleaning up, etc.); a pastor sharing his dreams for the Church; emphasis and public praise for disciple-making and discipleship; a new music team revived and publicly recognized and valued as a positive uniting activity; personal visits to every member and prospect; practiced evangelism through community events; initiation of new members class. There are many more, but you get the idea of new nudges that create a positive response within the fellowship and with its prospects.

Facilitator/Catalyst: Give your people some tools and then get out of the way and let God work! Stop looking for plug and play solutions (programs) and start looking for ideas that will work in your setting. Stop asking God to bless your ideas only after you have thought it all out and then just finally remembered to ask for his blessing, instead of asking for His guidance from the beginning.

Transformational Leader/Change Agent: The best way to confront momentous troubles in a congregation may be faced and overcome by a single solitary confident unrelenting leader. The best solution either to a predicament or a long-term issue that threatens the well-being of any church is understanding the issue and the need for a change agent. The transformational leader has the ability to anticipate resistance and sabotage. They can tell the difference between content and process (content is the stuff people are arguing about, process is the emotional reality).

Coach for Success: Understand that your methodology will look different than mine! As a coach, you must teach the importance of having persistence and a willingness to remain calm in the midst of various degrees of turmoil. The ability to stay connected with everyone during these hard times is part of coaching your congregation for success. They are watching you and your ability (or lack thereof) to be an anxiety shock absorber and display healthy emotional Teflon as you lead the church through the revitalization course of action.

Cheerleader/Energizer: Everybody at one time or another needs a little encouragement and public recognition for their efforts! Each time I enter into another church revitalization project and begin working with a new church or set of churches in a specific area, I think back to what we have previously discussed and I have affectionately called "The NUDGE List". Remember when you were a kid and one of your parents gave you praise and encouragement to get you back to your homework assignment? It was a gentle nudge. Churches that are falling back into becoming legacy churches often need the nudge into the beginnings of church revitalization in a similar way! Energizers are great at giving gentle nudges.

Manager/Director: Think about ideas and ways that will send a message to the community that you are doing a new thing. If you are the pastor, think about ways you can share the dream using short-term, mid-term, and long-range ideas and goals for renewal and revitalization. As the leader, stop trying to do so much alone. Impatient revitalization leaders are pushing too hard and seeking quick fixes over steady wins.

Intentional Growth Ambassador: Numerical growth is the least certain mark of church revitalization and renewal. Yet the local church is perceived as not growing without numerical growth. In church revitalization, growth and health do not come to pass by accident. You as the leader must be intentional about both. Churches that are revitalized first begin with a spiritually revitalized laity. If your growth is to be measured in people becoming involved in various ministries inside and outside of the church, then the various ministry teams must become easy to join and you must be able to make ministry simple, not complicated! I did not pay enough attention to this in one of my revitalization experiences and it almost cost us. Thank God that we began to pay more attention to visitation and follow-up.

Caregiver: Revitalization of churches is often very much similar from one church to another and yet often very much different in many ways! Hurting people are not healthy people. Unhealthy people make for an unhealthy church. We need to bring people to health before we can begin to renew the church. Caregivers are wired in ways that will assist you in working towards health. They are glue that keep your participants together and engaged. If you are going to succeed in church revitalization the church must stop allowing a small vocal minority to dictate what the church will or will not do! Every church begins its revitalization at a different place simply because every church is at a different place. Utilize your caregivers to help keep the place firmly connected and glued as one.

Partner/Friend: Everything that must be done in revitalization cannot be done in two or three hours on Sunday! Remember this: I (you) must change and grow if the church is going to change and grow. Stop doing the basic 3-5 years of ministry over and over in 3-5 places for your ministry career. Revitalization begins with you the lead pastor! Learn from others early and often. A pastor must earn the love and respect before he will earn the right to lead in renewal. Be a friend and partner. It is difficult for the laity to feel connected with a supported by a pastoral recluse.

Visionary: Having a vision for leading a church through the change that is needed in order to un-stick a stuck church is necessary for a visionary revitalization leader. Communicate early and often with the church how the revitalization procedure will take place and how it will be implemented. Prepare yourself spiritually as the visionary and then prepare your leaders spiritually. Then finally, you can begin preparing your church spiritually! Seek out God's guidance and power! Church revitalization is not about finding the "magic pill" or "sure to succeed" programming. It is more about discovering God's vision for the church and practicing it. Don't simply force your vision but instead help a congregation discover their vision for themselves.

When you turn the eyes of your church from inward focus to outward focus, then you are aligning your vision where Jesus can bless you.

CHAPTER THREE
The Re-Visioning of the Church

This pillar can be challenging, but certainly not as hard as the descending order of decline that will eventually lead to the *Restarting* pillar of revitalization! Have you ever seen a church that once was alive and vital begin to lose its focus and drive for the cause of Christ? That is a church that needs to work on its *Re-visioning* strategy! A good *Re-Visioning* strategy works to help churches dream new dreams and accomplish new goals that lead towards re-growing a healthy church. This strategy is designed for a weekend retreat tailor-fitted to foster a sense of ownership and teamwork related to discovering a shared vision for the church.

Understanding the critical milestones necessary for a new vision will help foster healthy church practices that might have been lost. Something as simple of achieving an identified goal of some sort can begin to launch a church back into a *Re-Visioning* strategy. Something as simple and dangerous as the Lord's children taking an ill-advised rest that resulted in a slowing or stalling of the momentum into a maintenance mentality can cause a church to become stuck.

The Smyrna Church was the church which received the Crown of Life.[31] Being faithful as individual believers as well as individual churches amidst persecution is found as a central truth in the second portion of Revelation Chapter Two. Smyrna

---

[31] C.f. Revelation 2:8-11.

was a bitter place for the Christian believers as the large Jewish population bitterly opposed Christianity. When Domitian (81–96 a. d.) issued an edict declaring the worship of the emperor suddenly, all of those except the Jewish population were required to worship him all across the Roman Empire. Domitian exempted the Jews from this proclamation. The Jewish residents did not desire to see those Christians in Smyrna receive the same exemption and religious freedom. No words of indictment are given to the congregation in Smyrna! They may not have enjoyed the endorsement of men, but they certainly received the acclaim of God. The Lord did give them sincere words of admonition as they faced increased suffering: *"Do not be afraid."* The church at Smyrna was facing increasing persecution and spiritual warfare. It costs to be dedicated to Christ today and Smyrna was an example of such cost. The great truth regarding revitalization and renewal found within this portion of scripture is that as one endures persecution, we are encouraged to continue being faithful, understanding that while more oppression may come upon us as believers, our eternal inheritance is secured.

God's rule over history provides a basis of comfort to the church, which is suffering economic hardship because of Jewish slander. Though, its members' faithfulness in the face of such affliction demonstrates their spiritual riches *"I know thy works."* Such spiritual wealth in the midst of economic poverty is a trait not untypical of believers in exile on the earth.[32] This is in contrast to rich, godless "earth-dwellers" who are poor in faith, which the church at Laodicea was on the threshold of becoming.[33] G. K. Beale in his commentary declares:

"From what we know of late first-century Asia Minor we can speculate about how these Christians were being persecuted. Until the latter part of the first century Christianity enjoyed a degree of protection under the umbrella of Judaism, which was tolerated by Rome. The Jews were not forced to worship Caesar as a god, but allowed to offer sacrifices in honor of emperors as rulers and not as gods (see further below on 2:24–25). But after the Neronian persecution Christianity came under suspicion, since new religions were not acceptable in the empire. And Jews, who sometimes had no qualms in semi-revering other deities along with their OT God, often were only too willing to make the Roman authorities aware that the Christians were not a Jewish sect."[34]

The detailed charges of Jews before government authorities were probably that Christians were upsetting the peace of the *status quo*, that they were not a bonafide Jewish sect, and that these Christians refused to worship Caesar as Lord.[35] The mention of

---

[32] C.f. 2 Corinthians 6:10; 1 Corinthians. 1:26–29.

[33] C.f. Revelation 3:17–18.

[34] Beale, 239-45.

[35] Cf. John 19:12; Acts 24:1–9.

persecution by the Romans (v.10) directly following that of Jewish slander conforms to historical reports[36] of Jews allying with and encouraging Romans and Gentiles to oppress Christians.[37] Kendell H. Easley says this "note condemns the Jews who met for worship in Smyrna. Because they were slandering the Christians, their meeting had become a *"synagogue of Satan"*[38] rather than a synagogue of God."[38] Our struggles are not with flesh and blood, but with the enemy, Satan, who uses people to achieve his purposes. The allegation is just as those in Smyrna who claimed to be God's people, the Jews who proved by their actions they were not worthy of the name. So those who claim to be God's people, the Christians, can prove by their actions to be the church of the living Lord. If there is a key truth regarding church revitalization and renewal found in this section, it is at the close of verse ten, *"be faithful, even to the point of death."* The persecuted Christians in Smyrna were not assured freedom from persecution. They were guaranteed something much greater, which was the grace to withstand the afflictions they faced without fear. They also received a pledge from the almighty, that as the one who died and rose again to life, Christ would bring them through to receive the *"crown of life."*

---

[36] E.g., Acts 13:45, 50; 14:2–7, 19; 17:5–9; 1 Thessalonians. 2:14–16.

[37] Beale, 239-45.

[38] Easley, 36-38.

The Smyrna Christians were overcomers and they had nothing to fear. They would be escorted into glory wearing crowns.

Re-visioning focuses the declining church on the future. "Vision is the 'What'—the picture of the future we seek to create".[39] As one seeks to re-vision the dying church, a godly vision can create a self-fulfilling prophecy. The church revitalizer's God-given vision should be challenging and stretching as it calls the people of God together in faith. Re-visioning visions face the present reality head-on. Re-visioning has a vision as a photograph of what the future might be. Kouzes and Posner say: "Visions are statements of destination, of the ends of our labor; they are therefore future-oriented and are made real over different spans of time."[40] Churches stuck in the past often are more focused on a romanticized past, or they start sinking in the messiness of the present quicksand the church is experiencing. The re-visioning of the church looks beyond the future that God seeks to create for your revitalizing church.

Andy Stanley says, "Visioneering is a process. Sometimes it is a painful process. Because of the time required, it can be agonizing. But it is a process that yields a product worth every bit of the agony along the way. You cannot rush the development of a child in the womb, so we cannot rush the development of a

---

[39] Fifth Discipline, p. 223.

[40] Kouzes and Posner, Leadership Challenge, p. 100.

vision...Immature visions are weak. They rarely make it in the world."[41]

Aubrey Malphurs gives the church revitalizer some coaching tips in the process of developing vision. He says:
1. Begin by asking over and over the question, "What do I see?"
2. Pray because prayer is vital to the process.
3. Think big, outside the lines, off the page.
4. Brainstorm verbally and in writing, reserving evaluation of the ideas until later.
5. Question the dream with these questions: Is it clear? Challenging? Does it create a picture in my mind? Is it futuristic? Are you convinced it must be? Is it a God-sized vision?
6. Demonstrate patience because visionizing takes time.[42]

Kouzes and Posner pen: "Leaders inspire a shared vision. To enlist people in a vision, leaders must know their constituents and speak their language. Leadership is a dialogue, not a monologue. Leaders speak to people's hearts and listen to their heartbeats because in the final analysis, shared visions are simply about common caring."[43] There is a difference between compliance with a vision and commitment to making the vision reality. People become committed to

---

[41] Stanley, Andy. *Visioneering*, p. 20.

[42] Malphurs, A. *Ministry Nuts and Bolts*, pp. 120, 121.

[43] Leadership Challenge, pp. 11, 132.

organizations where they feel they are valued as persons and cared for. Senge warns, "A vision can die if people forget their connection to one another...One of the deepest desires underlying shared vision is the desire to be connected, to a larger purpose and to one another."[44] There is much discussion in our culture about empowerment of people. Senge warns that without a commonly shared vision empowerment does not work. It only increases stress in people's lives and a burden on leadership to maintain direction.

Re-visioning expresses itself in images and pictures. It pursues reality from God's perspective. George Barna declares: "Vision for ministry is a clear mental image of a preferable future imparted by God to his chosen servants and is based on an accurate understanding of God, self and circumstances. Vision is a picture held in your mind's eye of the way this could or should be in days ahead."[45] As the church revitalizer leading the church re-visioning effort, take a moment and close your eyes. Do you see the clear picture of God's preferred future for your church? If not, keep praying and meditating, as one's clearest visions are often the direct result of eyes wide shut and mouth as well. Allow God to display a panoramic of His glorious direction of what your church could be in the near future. A panorama of your revision strategy becomes crisp and well-defined. Now open your eyes and get to work totally relying on the Lord each and every day.

---

[44] Fifth Discipline, p. 230.

[45] Barna, *Power of Vision*, pp. 28, 29.

CHAPTER FOUR
The Renewing of the Church

Church Renewal is the forth pillar of the seven pillars of Church Revitalization process. Often the church simply needs to get back to that which was working and get back on track. When that is needed a careful renewal strategy needs to be planned and carried out. Renewing a congregation becomes much harder than the refocusing, re-visioning and revitalization process. Not everyone who works in church renewal is wired the exact same way and it is important to understand each congregation's individual needs rather than trying to make one size fit all! There is no magic pill in church revitalization. Far too much writing on church growth of the 1980's was designed in a one size fits all "Bigger is Better" model and while it may not have been the only cause for declining numbers in our churches, it certainly contributed! It is vital that you prepare the laity for the work of church renewal as well as yourself. Communicate early and often with the church how the renewal process will take place and how it will be implemented. Prepare yourself spiritually and then prepare your leaders spiritually. Then begin preparing your church spiritually for renewal! A *Church Renewal Weekend* is a great way to start. Church renewal is not about finding the magic medication or treatment to get growing. It is more about discovering God's vision for the church and practicing it for the long haul. The utilization of a Church Renewal weekend works well to draw God's people back towards health and vitality.

The Church at Thyatira can be identified and

labeled as a corrupted unrepentant small community church.[46] It is interesting to note that the longest message to the seven churches of Asia Minor was sent to the smallest community. When one considers that this tiny community was the least consequential city of the entire group of Asian churches, the message delivered must be of such importance to the church of its day as well as the church of tomorrow that the relevance must not be missed. The spiritual battle that is waged within Thyatira is a strong parallel to the battle to be waged in the end times.[47] Jesus Christ is called within this passage *"The Son of God"* and it is the only time in the Book of Revelation that this phrase is utilized. John had to convey a message of severe warning and judgment to this congregation, which explains the description of the Lord as *"One whose eyes are like a fiery flame"* and *"whose feet are like fine bronze."*

Thyatira was a military town and an economic center with many trade guilds. As observed in previous messages to churches wherever trade guilds were instituted, idolatry and immorality were almost always present. Both were great enemies of the early church. In Thyatira each of its trade guilds were devoted to a patron god or goddess, and social events centered on their worship. The pressure for Christians to participate in this idolatrous lifestyle for both monetary and communal reasons like the two previous churches

---

[46] Revelation2:18-29.

[47] C.f. Revelation 14-18.

of Pergamum and Smyrna was excessive. The letter to Thyatira is the longest of the seven messages and stands as the centerpiece of the entire seven. Thyatira was some thirty miles southeast of Pergamum and was located on the Lycus River.

It was a busy church within this city. Thyatiraians were very busy carrying out sacrificial ministry for the sake of others. Additionally, their works were growing and characterized by faith, love, and patience; so the church at Thyatira was not guilty of mere religious activity. The *"works"* for which this church is first recognized are not mere general deeds of Christian "service" but are works of persevering witness to the outside world.[48] That this is explicitly meant is apparent from the fact that when "love," "faith," and "endurance", especially "endurance and faith," appear elsewhere within the Book of Revelation, they nearly always denote persevering witness. In contrast to the Ephesus church, the phrase *"your last works are greater than the first"* in reference to the Thyatira church, is a point of contrast where the Ephesus church's works were described as whose *"first works"* of public testimony and witness were greater than their last works of witness.[49] The Lord encourages the church at Thyatira to witness to the outside world.

Yet the church was not all blessings and benevolence, there was corruption and an un-

---

[48] Beale, 270.

[49] C.f. Revelation 2:5.

repentant spirit within the church. The Lord found much to uncover and censure in the Christian assembly at Thyatira. No amount of loving and sacrificial works can compensate for lenience of evil. The church was sanctioning a false prophetess to sway the membership and lead them into compromise. *"You tolerate the woman Jezebel"* was declared. It is not very likely that this woman was actually called *"Jezebel,"* since such an infamous name would not be given to a child at birth. The name is symbolic: Jezebel was the idolatrous queen who enticed Israel to add Baal worship to their religious ceremonies.[50] The seductive teaching of Jezebel was similar to the "doctrine of Balaam" that the Lord condemned in the church of Pergamos (2:14). She taught believers how to compromise with the Roman religion and the practices of the guilds, so that Christians would not lose their jobs or their lives.

It is thought-provoking to compare the churches at Ephesus and Thyatira. The Ephesian church was weakening in its love yet faithful to judge false teachers; while the people in the church at Thyatira were growing in their love but were too tolerant of false doctrine. Both extremes must be shunned within the church. "Speaking the truth in love" is the biblical balance.[51] Not only was the church at Thyatira accepting of evil, but it was unashamed and unwilling to repent. The Lord allowed the false prophetess time

---

[50] C.f. 1 Kings 16–19.

[51] C.f. Ephesians 4:15.

to repent, yet she rejected the opportunity. The Lord then allowed her followers the opportunity to repent, yet they also rejected the opportunity. His eyes of fire had searched out their thoughts and motives, and He would make no mistake. It is further revealing that the Lord threatened to use the entire church of Thyatira as a grave illustration to *"all the churches"* not to allow evil to infiltrate one's church. Jezebel and her spiritual children who have committed themselves to her false teaching would be sentenced to tribulation and death. God would judge the false prophetess and her followers once and for all.

Not everyone in the congregation was unfaithful to the Lord, and as such the Lord had a special word for them. They had detached themselves from the false doctrine and compromising practices of Jezebel and her followers. Without much hoopla the Lord simply challenges them to *"hold fast to what you have"* and resist the evil *"till I come."*[52] The compromising people in Thyatira were following *"the deep things of Satan,"* which would lead to darkness and death. The Lord's overcomers would share the *"Morning Star."*[53] How heartbreaking it is when a local church progressively leaves behind the faith and loses its witness for Christ. It is not just the lost who need to repent, but also disobedient believers. If we do not repent and deal with the sin in our lives and in our churches, the Lord may judge us and remove our lampstand.[54]

---

[52] C.f. Revelation 3:3; 16:15; 22:7, 17, 20.

[53] C.f. Revelation 22:16.

[54] C.f. Revelation 2:5.

Recreating the Mindset of the Members in the Renewing Church

Changing the mindset of the residual membership can often be very difficult. Senior adults occupy most of these restart candidate churches for whom change is often hard to come by. Until the church is ready to make drastic changes, it is useless to become involved. There are thousands of churches like this all over America: Some are Baptists, others are Methodists, even in the Assembly churches you can find them, Presbyterians, the Lutherans have them, Congregational, Christian, and many others, waiting for a mission-minded congregation to get involved in offering "new life." There is a tremendous need to recreate the mindset of the remaining member in renewing church.

One startling phenomena is that there are churches today that, as the laity begin to depart this life, often see nothing wrong with taking the church to the grave as well. Their motto could be: Would the last one alive, please turn the lights off! That was never part of God's plan for the very thing for which He gave up His life.

For the last 20 years, there has been a great deal of focus around the world on evangelism through church planting. Tens of thousands of people are coming to Christ each day around the world. Thousands of new churches are planted every week. We thank God for this spectacular growth!

However, there has not been corresponding attention given to the revitalization and renewal of our churches on the home front during this time. Consequently, today we have an increasing deficit of church revitalizers and a shortage of committed renewal leaders within our existing churches! As more and more Godly men are going into church planting, we have a crisis of pastors and ministry leaders seeking to lead the declining church out of its challenges and obstacles. We need new leaders and better-trained leaders in the area of church revitalization and renewal.

But hear me in this, if it were just about making a better leader, we have so many Christian leadership groups training and individuals going to weekly or monthly meetings for just this, and yet the pace of decline has not been slowed by building a better ministry leader to serve as pastor and shepherd. Clearly, our conventional methods and established approaches of leader development simply have not delivered either the quantity or quality of leaders that today's plateaued or rapidly declining churches need. We cannot keep building leaders the same way by merely trying to do it faster and on a larger scale.

It would be careless and irresponsible for us to simply rejoice in the great harvest of souls that is happening today through the planting of churches without addressing the issue of the development of Church Revitalizers for our churches across the world! If we do not take this seriously and address the issue of plateau and declining churches in a generation or two much of today's glorious harvest may be lost. More of the same will not do! We need to transform the way today's church revitalizers are trained.

CHAPTER FIVE
The Reinvention of the Church

This fifth pillar of Church Revitalization deals with the tools and techniques necessary to assist the church when it is essential to reinvent itself to an ever changing community. Churches, church leaders, church members, and stressed communities fail for many reasons, but perhaps the most common reason it that they fail to reinvent themselves. When a church experiences a shift in the community makeup, often there will be - to various degrees - the need to redevelop a new experience for those who make up the new context! New experiences must replace old experiences. New practices likewise will replace old practices. A church that is experiencing the need for reinvention must take seriously the need and make the commitment for reinventing itself, revaluing itself, reforming itself, and reinvigorating itself to fit the new context. When pastors, deacons, and church leaders rest on former successes rather than driving decisive transformation, they usually uncover much too late that they have lost their position of favor in the community they were called to serve and some other church has stepped in and taken the advantage. What is often left is a mere image of what the church was in the past and a compulsion to simply support the status quo of the past as the church begins to draw further away from the Lord's intention and call to the community.

The Church in Philadelphia is the church which thankfully is everywhere within the Western Hemisphere. It is a serving church that is holding on faithfully.[55] Faithful churches are abundant today and God is to be praised. The church in Philadelphia was one, that had a vision to reach a lost world, and as a result of this great vision the Lord God set before them an *"open door that no one is able to close."* Their great love for a lost world and their desire to reach unbelievers with the gospel is why the Lord declares that no one will be able to close their door. Our New Testament speaks to an *"open door"* as an opportunity for doing the work of ministry.[56] It is an open door of spiritual usefulness for the work of evangelization.[57] The church at Philadelphia was given a wonderful opportunity for ministry.

Philadelphia was situated in a strategic place on the main route of the Imperial Post from Rome to the East, and thus was called "the gateway to the East." It was located 40 miles southeast of Sardis and like the Sardis community, faced the long-term effects of the A.D. 17 earthquake, as did these community dwellers. Attalus Philadelphus, who was the king of Pergamos, built Philadelphia.[58]

---

[55] C.f. Revelation 3:7-13.

[56] C.f. Acts 14:27; 1 Corinthians 16:9; 2 Corinthians 2:12; Colossians 4:3.

[57] Jamieson, et al., Revelation 3:7–14.

[58] Ibid.

Philadelphia sat on a geological fault, and it was destroyed by a severe earthquake that also destroyed Sardis and ten other cities. As a result, the inhabitants planned for the event of future quakes. Nothing is known of the church at Philadelphia, yet the Apostle Paul connected these inhabitants to his ministry in Ephesus. It was also called "little Athens" because of the many temples in the city. The church was certainly located in a place of tremendous opportunity. The connection of this Church with Jews there causes the letter to it to have an Old Testament flavor in its imagery.[59]

Yet in the midst of opportunity there were challenges. At least two are found in this passage and are reminders of obstacles often faced in the revitalization of churches. The first challenge was their lack of strength as seen in John's declaration *"Because you have limited strength."* The Lord provides the church in Philadelphia, which is weak, God's abundance of power to rely upon so the world might see and give God all of the glory and praise. A faithful church it seems but with a small group of congregants. They were keeping God's Word as seen in the reference *"have kept My word"* and they were not afraid to bear witness of the Lord Jesus as John declares they *"have not denied my name."* When a church is faithful in the call of God and His commands, size really does not matter.

---

[59] Jamieson, et al., Revelation 3:7–14.

A second challenge and obstacle was found in the Jewish opposition in Philadelphia. The leaders of the Jewish synagogue excluded Jewish believers from worshipping in the synagogue. In the midst of the challenges, the Lord gives three declarations or promises to those of the church in Philadelphia. First, he says that he will take care of their enemies when he declares: *"I will make them come and bow down at your feet, and they will know that I loved you."* An emphasis for revitalization and principle would be that God will take care of our battles if we keep our lives focused on his work. Secondly, God will keep them from the tribulation. *"Because you have kept My command to endure, I will also keep you from the hour of testing that is going to come over the whole earth"* (v.10). John then adds that the Lord *"will come quickly"* to finish this declaration. Christ will show his faithfulness to the Christians in Philadelphia in the immediate future *because* they have been faithful witnesses to Him in the past.[60] The final declaration and promise to the believers in the church of Philadelphia is *"I will make him a pillar in the sanctuary of My God, and he will never go out again."* God is going to honor their steadfastness and commitment to the gospel. The Lord desires for us to be faithful pillars, and any church working towards revitalization and renewal needs a committed core of these types of individuals. Part and parcel for the work of

---

[60] Beale, 283-96.

revitalization is the ability to realize if God opens a door we are to work aggressively while there is still time. If the Lord closes a door of opportunity, we must wait patiently. Both require faithfulness to see past the obstacles and seek the opportunities.[61] Preservation is a mark of church revitalizers and the church in Philadelphia though small had its share.

Archeologically thought-provoking among the Seven Churches of Asia Minor is the church that still stands straight. One single column still is standing on site. Perhaps a pillar of honor representing a still open door towards evangelization and revitalization is Philadelphia proudly holding on and faithfully serving the Lord Jesus.

The most successful church turnarounds make reinvention a regular part of their ministry strategy. Transformation demands an ongoing process of re-discovery and imagination. As the church revitalizer, it is your responsibility to make the reinvention of your church a top priority. If your governance and organization structures in your church have become enamored by its own triumphs, your job is to introduce at every level that same inspired hunger that launched your church in the first place. When it comes to reinvention of the church, beginning is the toughest part of the task, but it is also the most

---

[61] C.f. 1 John 2:28.

important. With the warp speed of the space ship Enterprise, our world rushes by most declining churches because they fail to observe that swiftness wins. New ideas given by God are often moments of divine giftedness and pass by most dying churches, because while the church is fleshing out every possible scenario, the opportunity has passed them by while they are still meeting to think about things instead of taking action.

Reinvention of the local church differs from turning around a church. Many church members think they are interchangeable when nothing could be further from the truth. The characteristics of each are different, as a church turnaround is usually reactionary in nature. It positions itself to look backward at the past glories and not future possibilities. It is a response to the crushing challenges which these churches allowed to happen by indecision until it was almost too late. Turnaround churches seek survival while reinvention churches seek a glorious future of new commitments, new relationships, and new energies supported by a new community of church members desiring a high impact church over a no impact church. A church's effort for turnaround is reactionary and shortsighted, usually driven by an immediate need for survival. It is more about what visitors and new prospects can do for you not what you as a church can do for them. Innovation is not the norm in a turnaround. New ideas are often placed on the back burner or put on hold forever. Leaders of the just-keep-us-open movement of turnaround may crush church budgets, reduce minister's pay, blame the staff for the churches failures and put anything and everything on hold. New ideas are frowned upon and those who are the creative thinkers in the church and who could help the church are so crushed that eventually they quietly leave only to talk about the rank and files' unwillingness to do new things. In this scenario, you are memorialized in your mire of mundaneness. You have shredded any opportunity of new growth and advancement, and by the time a turnaround is recognized as necessary, it is often too late.

The only way to ward off the decay of rapid decline and continual stagnation is to practice ongoing reinvention as the church revitalizer. Change is inevitable. Even if you do nothing, there will still be change as you eventually die as a church. The sooner you lead the effort of reinvention as the church revitalizer in your church, the better your church's chance of existence.

Six Methodologies of the Reinvention Servant

Study any supremely successful organization or individual, and you will encounter a consistent theme. These methodologies for church reinventors run contrary to maintain-the-status-quo, stuck-in-the-past church leader. Let's consider these methodologies of church reinvention:

You must let go of the past daily. Pastors just can't live in the past anymore. You must honor the past but you can't live in it. If you do, you will be shackled with worries and fail to ever take a stand and start moving.

Be bold and brave, while courageously leading the church reinvention effort. "In with the new" is a great way to develop a much-needed sense of synergy and excitement for the revitalization effort of reinvention. Brave leaders lead boldly and implant a spirit of reinvention in the church by allowing any and all ideas to be voiced regularly. Celebrate renewal through reinvention and keep your people looking up towards heaven not down at their shoes.

If you at first don't succeed, then try again. I played baseball as a kid and I quickly learned that I was not going to get a hit every time. I had more misses at basketball then I did points. Setbacks are often your solutions to the future. We face them every day, so allow failure to be part of your reinvention process. Even you as the church revitalizer can't score a touchdown on every play, so embrace trial and error and never give up.

Run towards the runners. Stop playing it safe and start breaking through negativity by reaching out to those who are moving and not hiding in a cocoon. Stand up, stand firm, and stand out from the crowd of naysayers and work with the runners every day for church reinvention.

See the future and seize it. Reinventing a church is a challenging process. Face the reality; it is hard work! If you are not up to it, get out of the ministry of revitalization altogether. There is no room for lazy church revitalizers in God's army of individuals working to revitalize a dying church. Dream big and dream a little more until you have dreamed the biggest dream of your life for the cause of reinventing a local church who desperately needs to seize the day.

Success in church reinvention comes with a chilly greeting. Not everyone is going to be happy that you saved the church through your obedience to the Lord. There are difficult people, lazy people, mean people, and negative people in many of the churches that are dying. Serve them anyway. Frigid people need to get to heaven and it is up to you to lead them there. Be one who knows how to say "Yes" because there are many in the church that only know how to say "No." Overcome the chill of the unwilling and lead your church towards the reinvention of itself. It will warm you up and it just might do it for all of your naysayers. I say it this way: *B the B.* Be the Blessing your church members need and refuse to allow a few who want to constrain you to do so.

CHAPTER SIX
The Restoration of the Church

This sixth area of Church Revitalization addresses the things a church and a minister must work through when circumstances necessitate a restoration process! These things include:

- Gaining a new and fresh understanding of the new prospect for the church, which is vital if success is in the church's future.
- Inspiring new prospects with a vision that is both compelling and motivational. Prospects seek to be inspired and not dragged down in the world in which we live.
- Meeting new needs in order to give you a restored place within the community where you seek to further minister.
- Become prospect driven during these days of transition. Look for new and unreached opportunities I which to minister.
- Remember if you try to do everything, you will end up doing nothing. Therefore, pick your greatest opportunities first and let the rest follow along later.
- Craft something that comes as a result of a community in flux. Look for ways to reconnect with the community where you once were firmly entrenched. Keep in mind you have been given a second chance, so don't blow it. Prayerfully seek the new things because it might be something you will be doing for a long long time!

The Church in Laodicea is like so many today as it is the self-sufficient apostate church.[62] Arrogance and a sense of self-sufficiency have been around for a long time. It is apparent in society and sadly also in the local church. Wealth often gets in the way of serving the Lord Jesus. Laodicea was well-known for its wealth and it had two specific industries, which brought it its wealth. It manufactured a distinctive eye balm for use in its flourishing medical center, as well as a glossy black wool cloth. Laodicea was located near Hierapolis, where there were famous hot springs, and Colossae, known for its pure, cold water. Hierapolis had hot medicinal waters; Colossae had cold, pure, refreshing water. Located 43 miles southeast of Philadelphia[63] eleven miles west of Colossae, six miles south of Hierapolis,[64] and 90 miles east of Ephesus, it was an important trade center. Laodicea served as a gateway to Ephesus, which was the entryway to Syria.[65] Formerly it was known as Diospolis the city of Zeus. Around 250 B.C. Antiochus II, the ruler of Syria, further extended his influence to the west as he conquered the city and renamed it in honor of his wife Laodice.[66] As were the previous two churches located in the earthquake zone, this city also lay in the regional

---

[62] C.f. Revelation 3:14-22.

[63] Simon J. Kistemaker, *New Testament Commentary: Exposition of the Book of Revelation*, (Grand Rapids, MI: Baker Books, 2001), 166.

[64] C.f. Colossians 4:13.

[65] Kistemaker, NTCR, 166.

[66] Ibid.

path. Due to the earthquakes Laodicea had to pipe in its water to the community. This was accomplished through a system of aqueducts, which feed the city. In seasons of draught it was vulnerable. In times of war their enemies could disrupt the flow of water into the city.

In Colossians 1:7 we learn that Epaphras perhaps planted the church at Laodicea.[67] Churches were also planted in Hierapolis and Colossae[68] during the Apostle Paul's three-year ministry in Ephesus. So foolish was the church that, as the Lord was about to tell them the truth about their spiritual condition, refused to believe His diagnosis. *"The Amen[69], the faithful and true Witness"* the Lord declares. God speaks truth, is truth, and conveys truth because He is the faithful and true witness. G.K. Beale concludes that the "self-description of Christ in this final letter emphasizes more explicitly than in Revelation 3:7 his role as a 'faithful witness,' which was first mentioned in Revelation 1:5."[70] Jesus is the faithful witness and those believers in the Laodicean church were

---

[67] C.f. Acts 19:8-10; 20:31.

[68] As believers in Jesus Christ, we have every reason to be "fervent in spirit" (Rom. 12:11). Fervent prayer is also vital (Col. 4:12). This Epistle is thought to have been written to the Laodicean Church by Paul (Col 4:16). It was as the Emmaus disciples listened to the Word that their hearts were warmed. Paul had directed that the letter to the Colossians be read by the Christians in Laodicea.

[69] C.f. Isaiah. 65:16.

[70] Beale, 296-301.

implicated for their ineffectiveness of faith. God does expect a level of competence as a believer and Christ follower. Was their witness nonexistent as so many are today, or was the finding of middle ground an offense to the Lord God who desires our witness? He continues, the three descriptions *"the Amen, the faithful and true"*[71] are not distinct but generally overlap in meaning to underline the idea of Jesus' faithfulness in testifying to his Father during his earthly ministry and his continuing as such a witness.[72]

Often in the area of church revitalization foolishness is accompanied by blindness to the real needs of the church and displays an unwillingness to face present realities. *"I know your works, that you are neither cold nor hot."* The church of Laodicea was without the stamina, strength, and staying power to spiritually press on for Christ. They had become worthless in their focus of self-sufficiency. *"I wish that you were cold or hot."* John declared that they have a lukewarm existence toward the Lord and it is repelling. A visual is in play here; the aqueducts usually delivered water to the city that was not cold and refreshing or warm and soothing. Members within this church were unaware of their need as they were more focused on their personal comfort, happy with complacency, and numb to the things around them. Feel the impact of falling into a cold iced creek in the winter and one would immediately feel the sensation. Put your feet

---

[71] C.f. Isaiah. 65:16.

[72] Beale, 296-301.

into a hot sauna and your senses would become alert, but the Christians in Laodicea were anything but alert. The church was self-regulating, self-satisfied, self-absorbed, and self-sufficient. Self-sufficiency is the fatal danger of a lukewarm state.[73] How often in church revitalization does there exist a difference of analysis? This church thought like so many today, that it was in a great situation only to find that the Lord had a different view. When a church rests in its financial pedestal it might just become blind in their spiritual health, which is never indicated by an economic pedestal.

The foolishly self-absorbed church displayed that they had lost their tenets and beliefs. While many looked upon themselves as rich, in fact they were the poorest spiritually of all the seven churches. This message to the Laodicean church reveals nothing of the Jewish presence, which could mean that their proclamation of the Gospel was of little threat to the Jews.[74] When a churches beliefs and spiritual convictions are replaced by pride, its ability to see its state in the Lord eyes is blinded. *"I am going to vomit you out of My mouth"* is God's declaration of the nausea and revulsion they bring. *"You are wretched, pitiful, poor, blind and naked,"* He declares. When churches beliefs are replaced by the perverted values of the business world, nausea will occur.

---

[73] Jamieson, et al., Revelation 3:14–21.

[74] Kistemaker, NTCR, 167.

The Laodiceans in church were displaying a loss of the original vision that launched that church. It had become accepting towards other religions. They were contented and relaxed in their wealth. Reality was blinded by their personal agendas. *"Listen, I stand at the door and knock. If anyone hears My voice and opens the door, I will come in to him and have dinner with him."* The Lord Jesus is standing right outside but the church at Laodicea just did not need Him. When a church gets so preoccupied with building its own little kingdom, the greater Kingdom with a heavenly concern for a dying lost world plays second fiddle to the self-absorption of the fickle and foolish. Their passivity led to their failure to press the message of Christ Jesus. They had no interest in giving witness and serving for the Lord. Advancement of the gospel in this congregation was lacking. *"I know your works"* the Lord declares in an implication that they were none.

Finally, the Church at Laodicea was *"naked"* in the eyes of God. Though the city was a place for wool manufacturing, these believers walked around fully clothed and yet they were uncovered and unprotected. In the Old Testament, nakedness meant to be defeated and humiliated.[75] Clothed in an array of fine garments was not their real need. They needed to be clothed in the eternal forgiveness of Christ Jesus. God's grace and righteousness was in need. Notice in the passage that the Lord only offers the invitation to those few. *"If anyone hears"* was not an offer to everyone in the

---

[75] C.f. 2 Samuel 10:4; Isaiah. 20:1–4.

church of Laodicea. They were an independent church that had wanted of nothing, but they were not abiding in Christ and drawing their power from Him. Even these concluding remarks, which speak to the basis for revitalization as an invitation to renewal, are offered to those believes who are already saved but have drifted. Individual repentance as well as corporate repentance is necessary in church revitalization.

It is God's nature to restore that which is broken, and He has demonstrated His power to restore many times. I can think of several examples from church history, beginning with the Protestant Reformation. However, the best witness to the work of God comes not from our history books, but from scripture itself. Scripture gives us an amazing record of God's work of restoration.

There are various ministry groups which offer help to individual pastors and clergy who are in need of restoration. I have chosen to list several below as a starting place for any who are struggling in this area as a minister:

Fallen Pastor: Finding Restoration in a Fallen World - http://fallenpastor.com

Affair Recovery online: www.AffairRecovery.com.

Restoring a Fallen Christian: http://www.fitlyspoken.org/restoring-a-fallen-christian/

Pastoral Restoration: The Path to Recovery: http://media.focusonthefamily.com/pastoral/pdf/PAS_Pastoral Restoration.pdf

CHAPTER SEVEN
The Restarting of the Church

The final Pillar of Church Revitalization is the hardest, and often only happens once the church's patriarchs and matriarchs have tried everything else they could think of to grow the church with no success! The challenge here is that most churches wait too long to enter into this area of revitalization and by the time they are willing to utilize this strategy they have sucked out all the life within the church and it is no longer a viable candidate for this effort. When a sick church no longer has the courage to work through the various issues that led to its poor health, it is usually identified as being on life support and in need of a restart. This type of church has been flat lined and is just holding on by means of its legacy and the faithful few who attend. The Restarting Strategy (also known as a Repotting strategy) is intended for an unhealthy church that is ready to return to a time of growth and to engage in a renewed vision that is demonstrated through ample demonstrations of hope. The restart based church revitalization model is being used all across North America. Any group planting churches or working in the area of church revitalization should have a restart strategy if it is going to be a wise steward. A critical point from the start of this process is a complete change of leadership and direction; it is a must for this revitalization model to be successful. Lyle Schaller reminds us that 85,000 evangelical churches are running with fewer than 50 attendees on Sunday morning. Being aware of their "critical" condition, however, is not enough. They must become convinced they need "major" surgical treatment. Terry Tolleson says that "some churches need help that goes beyond the work of revitalization"[76] and "the process of restart may offer a new paradigm for reclaiming churches."[77]

One church I have worked with still believes that they still have more to offer though their decline has been meteoritic, and yet they refuse to allow a restart to take place. Are you a declining church with under 50 participants each week? Have you lost the critical mass necessary to revitalize your church? Are the few visitors you do have not coming back? Is your reputation with the community at an all-time low? At the end of the month are there more bills than tithes and offerings? Thousands of churches in every denomination are faced with these questions. According to Ken Priddy, "Churches are dying at an alarming rate."[78] He further points out that: "One of two arguments is frequently presented as a rationale for not adopting Restart as a strategy. The first states that Restart is difficult and unlikely to succeed, and that a better strategy would be to close the church and to invest its assets in church planting. The second would be to allow the church to die a natural death and then to invest its assets in church planting. Each

---

[76] Terry Tolleson, "Restart: An Alternative for Reclaiming Churches" (D.Min. diss., Gordon-Conwell Seminary, 1999), Abstract.

[77] Ibid., 10.

[78] Kenneth Earl Priddy, "Restarting the Dying Church" (D.Min. diss., Reformed Theological Seminary, 2001), 58.

of these positions is flawed."[79]

The Church at Sardis was perhaps the saddest of all of the churches, as it was the has-been, dying church.[80] Becoming comfortable within the church is an age-old problem that certainly was confronting the churches of Asia Minor. Compromise was becoming the order of the day and believers were being challenged to conform to the world rather than the Word of God. All the churches were facing the enticement to compromise and some of the churches such as Pergamum, Thyatira, Sardis, and Laodicea were surrendering to this enticement. Therefore, as Beale suggests, the exhortation to the church at Sardis to overcome is either an encouragement to continue standing strong against compromise or to stop compromising. [81] Sardis lay about fifty miles east of Ephesus and roughly 30 miles southeast of Thyatira. It was one of the oldest cities in Asia Minor and was founded around 1200 B.C. In A.D. 17 it was destroyed by an earthquake and was later rebuilt with the assistance of the Emperor Augustus. Sardis was at the junction of five main roads, which intersected within their city so it was a center for various forms of trade. Located on a plateau, the acropolis of Sardis was about 1,500 feet above the main roads. It was known for its manufacturing of woolen garments, but the days of

---

[79] Priddy, "Restarting the Dying Church," 124.

[80] C.f. Revelation 3:1-6.

[81] Beale, 270.

splendor were passed for both the city and the church at Sardis.

Alive in name only, the city, which in former times was vibrant and growing, now is a shadow of its former glory. Jesus challenged the church in Sardis to become a congregation with true spiritual life.[82] As an example towards revitalization and renewal the church of Sardis is a warning that living on past glories will not suffice. The Lord criticizes the vast group of followers in the church for their spiritual stupor. He challenges them to repent and return to their earlier spiritual sparkle.[83] The former movement that was happening within the church towards growth now was headed towards becoming a stone relic and monument to the past. Hope was still available, but if it dragged its feet much longer all hopes of revitalizing the church would be lost. The church at Sardis needed the life that only Jesus through the Holy Spirit could provide.[84] Churches who are living in past glories and seeking to muster up some form and function of previously effective programs will not always see new growth as a result. When man is behind programs rather than the Lord, doom and lack of transforming life are more in effect. The "has been" church here was frail in its existence, feeble in its function, foolish in its approaches, and fruitless in its form. While there was still a tiny remnant within the church that was alive, most of the following was conforming to the world

[82] Easley, 52.

[83] Ibid, 53-56.

[84] C.f. Ephesians 4:4.

over commitment in the faith. In light of revitalization and renewal, there are times when a church is dying and it appears to be the pastor's fault, however here there is not mention of removing the "*star*" and putting a new shepherd in place.

The Sardis church had no words of criticism and no words that challenged their doctrinal view. There was no mention of persecution from the community to the church as in other instances within the seven churches of Asia Minor. A point can be made that, unlike some of the others which were indeed facing persecution, had the church in Sardis become so comfortable conforming to the pagan world where they lived that their comfort was because they had yielded to the ungodly culture around them. The has-been church had lived in the past for so long it no longer felt like it could make a difference. The evangelistic force and gospel witness it once had appeared to be lacking as John writes his letter. In their journey toward decay, most has-been churches sometimes simply go to sleep and if they wake up at all they discover they are dead.

Historically, the community of Sardis had its citadel captured twice and each time it was due to the guards failing to stand up to their responsibilities. Historically relevant to this example in revitalization is that this church could have become so complacent about doing the work of ministry that like the citadel, it could have allowed the enemy to slip its way into the fellowship. The impression for the Church at Sardis is that the entire congregation lacked the aggressiveness necessary to continue its bold witness to the city. With the absence of any word about persecution and conflict the thought could arise fairly that the has-been church was motionless in its presentation of the gospel and sought peace at all cost over friction. Only in the churches of Sardis and Laodicea do we read of "no conflict" with foes within or without the Church. Not that either had renounced the appearance of opposition to the world; but neither had the faithfulness to witness for God by word and example,[85] so as to "torment them that dwelt on the earth."[86] The gospel was not advancing in this church and was viewed by the community as neither needed nor evangelistically daring enough to reach them with the gospel. Their decaying witness was exemplified by their decaying impact on the community it was called to reach.

The Lord signals his concern when he declares, *"Be alert and strengthen what remains."* The guards are sleeping and one of the initial steps towards revitalization in a has-been church is a realistic assessment that things are not what they ought to be. "Dead" cells cannot produce those that are live and reproducing. This assessment of their state of being here reveals that their condition is a figurative hyperbolic overstatement intended to emphasize the church's precarious spiritual state and the imminent

---

[85] C.f. Revelation 11:10.

[86] Jamieson, et al., Revelation 2:28–3:6.

danger of its genuine death.[87] Some of the challenges for revitalization and renewal seen in the Sardis church were that they needed to repair the situation, restore their witness, replace comfort with evangelistic compassion for the lost, and begin to reproduce other followers of Christ. Has-been churches lack the zeal to regain the charge and complete the task. These churches such as Sardis lack the faith to testify boldly and openly regarding Jesus. Those that do not are plateaued, dying or already dead. Spiritual lethargy had seeped into the fellowship at Sardis and it is still a challenge for churches today. G. K. Beale, in *The Book of Revelation: A Commentary on the Greek Text* states: Whereas the majority of the people in the church at Sardis had compromised by not bearing witness to their faith, there were still a few who had been faithful in the task. The fact that they had "not stained their garments," as had the rest, reveals that the manner in which most of the Sardian Christians were suppressing their witness was by assuming a low profile in idolatrous contexts of the pagan culture in which they had daily interaction.[88]

I will *"come as a thief in the night"* and judge the church at Sardis was the Lord's warning. The counterfeit character of individuals in our churches will be revealed at the last day when these individuals do not receive God's final reward of life eternal. The tiny remnant, which remained faithful in the church at

---

[87] Beale, 272-82.

[88] Ibid.

Sardis, was the future of the church's turnaround and ministry advancement. God gives a brief formula for revitalization when he challenges them to *"be alert,"* remain *"watchful,"* *"repent,"* *"remember"* the Word of God, *"complete"* the task of God and do what it declares. The inspiration in this passage for revitalization is there is not a church that is beyond hope so long as a remnant remains that is willing to strengthen those that stay and reach others with the gospel.

Memberships are Souring and the Ability to Reclaim Former Members has Ceased

It is no secret that the local New Testament church today is in a pickle! Memberships are souring and the ability to reclaim former members has become a thing of the past. The hard reality in North America is that most churches and most, if not all, denominations are in a state of decline. The membership within these churches and denominations is plateauing and what used to pass for involvement and activity within churches is deteriorating. While all of this is happening, the rank and file of the church appears powerless to assemble the strength that is needed to get the churches growing again. A small church can be defined as one in which the number of active adult members and the total annual undesignated budget are inadequate relative to the church's current organizational needs and expenses. It is a church struggling to pay its minister, heat or cool its buildings, and find enough people to assume leadership responsibilities to take the church into the future.

In 1990 an editor for the *Wall Street Journal* Wade Clark Roof published an editorial article entitled, "The Episcopalian Goes the Way of the Dodo," where he argued the decline of mainline denominationalism and its effect on Christianity.[89] With the turn of the twenty-first century, sustained growth within our churches is an intermittent exception while decline seems to be more of the pronouncement. The mainline denominations, to which Roof referred, are still in the midst of severe decline and serious deterioration. Stuck in the status quo, new wine cannot be poured into the same old wine skins of outdated mindsets. A new sense of urgency is required for lasting change. Change is required and the church in need of revitalization and renewal cannot escape change. Will we allow the church of America to become mirrors of the churches all across Europe that find themselves empty urns holding the obvious?

The need for training today's minister with the tools and skill sets necessary to combat this rampant plateau and decline is crucial. Most ministers coming out of our seminaries today lack preparation for the challenge of church revitalization and renewal. If the estimates are accurate that, at a minimum, 80 percent

---

[89] Wade Clark Roof, "The Episcopalian Goes the Way of the Dodo," *Wall Street Journal*, July 20, 1990.

or more of our churches are in need of revitalization, then it stands to reason that the majority of graduates from our seminaries are going to begin their ministries in the majority of these churches. Less than five percent of these graduates will actually be going to healthy churches. Existing ministers will pastor the healthy pool of churches that make up the twenty percent so the seminarian needs to prepare for the eventual challenge of revitalizing a plateaued or declining church.

Each year approximately 3,500 churches die in North America.[90] Within my own Southern Baptist Convention the annual death rate averages between seven and nine hundred![91] Studies have shown that churches typically plateau in attendance by their fifteenth year, and by year 35 they begin having trouble replacing the members they lose."[92] Only 7.3 % of small churches are growing in North America currently. Of the churches, which are fifty years old or older, only 9.2% are growing.

In North America, fifty to sixty churches close their doors every week. Among churches of all sizes, growing churches are rare! In fact, they only make up

[90] Warren Bird, "More Churches Opened Than Closed in 2006," *Rev Magazine*, July-August 2007, 68.

[91] *"Annual Change in the Number of Southern Baptist Churches 1973-2009"* Center for Missional Research, North American Mission Board, SBC. Alpharetta, Georgia.

[92] "Churches Die with Dignity" *Christianity Today* Jan. 1991, Vol. 36.

about "20 percent of our churches today. The other 80 percent have reached a plateau or are declining."[93] In a study of more than two thousand churches, David Olson revealed that 69 percent of our churches in America have reached a plateau or even worse are declining.[94] Jim Tomberlin and Warren Bird declare that "80 percent of the three hundred thousand Protestant churches in the United States have plateaued or are declining, and many of them are in desperate need of a vibrant ministry."[95] The majority of these churches have fewer than two hundred people in attendance and a large portion have fewer than seventy-five weekly.[96]

I would be the first to tell you that while difficult, a restart just might be your church's best chance to become a growing viable church once more. I have been working with churches and doing the work of restarting churches for more than twenty years now. It

---

[93] Stetzer, Ed and Warren Bird, *Viral Churches: Helping Church Planters Become Movement Makers* (San Francisco: Jossey-Bass, 2010), 60.

[94] David T. Olson, *The American Church in Crisis* (Grand Rapids: Zondervan Publishing, 2008), 132.

[95] Tomberlin, Jim and Warren Bird, *Better Together: Making Church Mergers Work* (San Francisco: Jossey-Bass, 2010), xvi.

[96] "Fast Facts." Hartford Institute for Religion Research. Retrieved from http://hirr.hartsem.edu/research/fastfacts/fast_facts.html#sizec ong (accessed 3/20/2011).

is not the easiest process but it is perhaps the one that affords you the greatest chance for complete turnaround and renewal. I am a Southern Baptist and as such I often share what I am learning within my own beloved denomination with the field of revitalization and renewal.

Growing the Kingdom by Giving Up

As church memberships become entrenched in senior citizen based populations, few options remain to keep the church going and often they are left with few choices as to what they can do. Here are the basic set of choices when you have allowed your critical mass to decline to such a state as to threaten the possible closure of your church:

- You can make the transition towards a totally bi-vocational pastor and staff.
- You can move towards morning services only and rent out your facility to a Church Planter in the evening.
- You can sell your land, which is in my opinion the worst thing you could do!
- You could begin to place a higher degree of responsibility on lay leadership to pick up the slack of not having a full-time pastor.
- You could try to keep doing the same thing you are doing and hope that things will change. (Remember that if you do what you have always done you will get what you have always gotten.)

It is important to realize that if you wait too long to make necessary changes and the membership continues to decline to less than fifty adult active members, which is known as *"Critical Mass,"* then you should deed the church over to the local association as a *Legacy Church* and allow such an organization to utilize the church for future ministries while assuming your bills and upkeep. This allows future restarts to win and keeps a missional presence in the geographical location of the former church.

A decision to close a church should never be made on the basis of any single sign outlined above, but taken as a whole they can provide church leaders with helpful insights as to the future potential of a church. Giving up the facilities to a group that will restart the church honors those who have sacrificed so greatly in the past for the cause of Christ. You can grow the Kingdom of God by being willing to let go instead of trying to hold on until that last one passes on into eternity.

The restart based church revitalization model is being used all across North America. Any group working in the area of church revitalization should have a restart strategy if it is going to be a wise steward. I had never sought to write a step-by-step process for doing a church restart. Yet so many have used these materials over the last twenty years, that it has become a better identified process. Sometimes I get kind nods of encouragement thanking me for the bold stance and unwavering advice offered within this strategy. And frankly, a few times I have been ripped apart by those not brave enough to consider such drastic steps to move their local church towards a new expression of health and vitality! The idea of a dying church taking the necessary steps of a restart in order to provide it the best chance for survival is not an easy idea to consider. For those who have been part of the setback, admitting that they have hurt the church is hard indeed. Those who will take over also have a challenge in that it will be under their watch that they seek to change those traits, now embedded within the local church, for the betterment and opportunity to turn around a church that is in rapid decline.

It is amazing to me today that many individuals that attend a dying church see nothing wrong biblically with allowing their church to die along with them. It is as if there is a secret message, which reads: "The last one alive, remember to turn the lights out!" Humorous? Possibly! Tragic for sure because the local church is the very thing for which Christ Jesus gave His life and yet we treat his local church with such irreverence that it is no wonder churches are dying all across the world. This restart strategy is a vital piece for anyone working in church revitalization efforts and for those who possibly lead church planting efforts. If the two disciplines could somehow just join forces at this point perhaps it could be the local church that ultimately wins. Change is going to happen within the small rapidly declining church and this strategy offers an opportunity for a turnaround that is working, has been working for decades, and needs to be reconsidered in light of the advancing decline and plateauing of our churches today.

Pastors and denominational workers who want to see a difference in their churches must commit themselves to making change happen. It was Dr. Henry Blackaby who said, "If you are going to join God, you must change. You cannot stay the same and work with God at the same time."

Statistics are Our Friends in Restarting Churches

LifeWay Christian Resources, a research arm within the Southern Baptist denomination, worked cooperatively with the Center for Missional Research from the North American Mission Board to conduct a study of churches' five-year change in total membership. The study reports that 28.1 percent of our Southern Baptist Convention churches are growing, 43.9 percent are in a state of plateau, and 28 percent are in decline.[97]

Another longitudinal series of studies were conducted by Bill Day, Associate Director of the Leavell Center for Evangelism and Church Health. Day also serves the New Orleans Baptist Theological Seminary as the Gurney Professor of Evangelism and Church Health, and in his sequential studies on church health and growth from 2003, 2007, and 2010, he reported that currently there are less than seven percent (6.8) of our SBC churches which are healthy growing churches. That means a mere 3,087 of our

---

[97] Annual Church Profile data, LifeWay Christian Resources, Nashville, TN. Compiled by: Center for Missional Research, North American Mission Board, Alpharetta, GA.

45,727 SBC churches are healthy.[98] Leonard Sweet states that the declining mainline church has faced a "double whammy of postmodernity and post-Christendom."[99]

The Time Is Right Now!

If there is going to be revitalization in American churches in the twenty-first century, the initial step must be taken immediately. Revitalization of our churches is not an insurmountable task. While we must start with re-encountering the divine and realizing any church that is revitalized or becoming revitalized is from the work of our Lord God, we must do our part to provide tools and methodologies for today's ministers to assist them with new practices and approaches that can help today's declining churches. Our churches must not remain in stained glass, red bricked, spire castles giving out apologies for lack of renewal or mixed gestures towards revitalization efforts.

The time for revitalization and renewal is now; sick and declining churches are all across America. Will the people of God be led like days of old when the shepherds of God boldly served the church of God and led His people to remember why they exist and to

---

[98] Bill Day. *The State of the Church in the S.B.C.* (New Orleans: Leavell Center for Evangelism and Church Health, 1/3/2012), C.f. Appendix Two.

[99] Leonard Sweet. *So Beautiful: Divine Design for Life and the Church* (Colorado Springs: David C. Cook, 2009), 20.

whom they belong? With such an absence of missionary mandates from our missionary agencies, the challenge is for the theological institutions across the convention to pick up the slack and prepare the new army of church revitalizers.

Some church revitalization restarts originate from the decline of others due to failure to remain on the threshold of community transitions. Sometimes our memories of how things use to be hinder us from seeing what we could become. Death is painful, but Jesus Christ can bring something new out of the sorrow.

When we are talking about a true "church revitalization restart," I am not referring to the typical small, struggling church that finds fresh life and growth, nor am I looking at mergers or relocation of existing churches. A church that is a candidate for a church revitalization restart has already sought advice from the local association leader or district leader about disbanding or is almost ready to disbanded. The church has dwindled down to about twenty or thirty survivors who are too tired to continue on. They no longer possess the critical mass necessary to get the church healthy again. The leadership that remains are too tired, too ineffective, and too small in number to bring about the changes it will take to make the turn. Those left are at the end of their rope and often want to make decisions that are unwise or lack any chance of success.

A church in need of a restart is a church that must have leadership and resources from outside of itself. Within these churches God often uses the local missions' leader or a district superintendent leader to help bring to life a church revitalization restart. These leaders will look for healthy churches to parent the restart for a time. When a parenting church or field partner seeks to aid a dying congregation with a solid revitalization strategy, reality must be squarely faced and decisions must be made that are often hard for the declining church. It is hard to admit sometimes, but the concept of letting the declining or dying church die is huge if you are going to restart it and make it a growing new work. For good healthy change, there needs to be a spiritual death for that former church. There is mixed opinion in the area of whether a church revitalization restart should close up for a time or continue on. I believe a significant case could and should be made for closing if not for even just a short time. To be fair, some say that a rebirth of vision is all that is needed. That may be too optimistic and in my individual experience too unrealistic as well.

The future of mainline churches is that they will be smaller and probably won't be able to afford a full-time pastor, which means that we are going to see more and more folks becoming "tent making" pastors who have a job outside of the church on top of their duties in the congregation. A lot of folks, including both people just coming out of seminary as well as current pastors, are not ready for this future. Mainline protestants are used to having full-time pastors in their churches. Individuals who are pastors or are going to be pastors unrealistically expect that they will have a nice full-time job.

Not Every Church is a Candidate for a Restart

Interestingly, many laymen often ask me if I think that their church could be a candidate for a restart. Usually they share in the need for their church to be revitalized. A series of questions frequently follows, and I will answer each and every single one of them. Once they wear out in asking questions, I ask one. That question is: "How willing are you and your lay leadership to let go of the controls of the church for the next three years and allow someone else to make the decisions necessary to restart your church?" One of two things happens at this point:

1. No Need to Bleed!
The first response is that the individual and his co-leaders see no need to make such a drastic decision. There is no real need to make those necessary decisions that will stop the bleeding of the exodus. After all they have been leading the church for over twenty years and see no reason to make this change despite the decline they are facing. Failure to admit ones' weakness and need for a restart is often the initial response. Their emphasis on former glories over present or future glories is a key to the polarization and "stuckness" they face.

As a layperson, you have more to do with the church in its present state then you often realize. Whether the congregation in which you belong is thriving or declining, it is ultimately up to you and your fellow members, and because of you and your fellow members. Pastors are called to equip the saints for the work of the ministry and they can certainly teach, inspire, train, lead, and inspire! But when the rubber meets the road, your church's health is a function of how you and your fellow members relate to one another, to the community in which the church is located, and to how they respond to God's leading within their lives. John 10:10 reminds us that Jesus said, "I came that you might have life, and have it abundantly." We need to be reminded that as laymen, we are the church! When a local church is spiritually journeying as a vibrant church:

- Church members willingly work together!
- The community finds hope from the church!
- There is a sense of belonging and togetherness!
- Members easily and frequently forgive others!
- Laity find individual and corporate sense of purpose!
- God's leading and direction is apparent to everyone!

Your pastor can be the greatest pastor and preacher, but his message only has the power to the extent that the people of God within the specific local church live it and practice it with each other!

2. Is There a Guide to Stop the Slide?

The other response is less common and happens when the leader himself asks how this happened and who would assist them in considering such an option.

The question was once asked this way, "Pastor is there a guide we can follow in order to stop the slide we are facing?" Some laymen desire to stop the near death throes of their dying church and take the drastic steps necessary to help it become healthy and vibrant once more. They are more concerned about the future needs by allowing the Lord to bring about a resurrection of life the way God wants over what man has become comfortable in.

The church dying or in rapid decline must face the hard realities and wrestle with the biblical passages dealing with reinvention, realignment, and restarting. Scriptures speak of the message of death and resurrection and for rapidly declining churches it is a testament that God can bring life out of something that was once dead. You do not begin in the Bible with new life. You begin with life, death, and being raised in newness of life. Rapidly declining churches often want to skip the journey and jump right to newness of life. Jesus is a fitting example of not missing the process necessary to embrace newness of life.

A Restart Churches Revitalization Lesson

When a local church refuses to trade its fear of closing the door for a desire to see life come back within the congregation, the church revitalization experience will end promptly as soon as the danger of death has been eliminated. What happens next may mean another recycle of decline until it is bad again. Churches only experience renewal when their people experience renewal! Unless a church's leadership wants renewal, it will not happen. There must be a commitment to lead the church towards revitalization. If not, nothing will be changed. Church renewal must shift from a few being interested to eventually a full effort of the entire congregation. Revitalization is not a secret journey but a public one.

Preachers of the Word are called by God and even with their giftedness, renewal will not happen unless the laity is willing to experience a new and better journey. If laity refuse to change, refuse to repent of unconfessed sins which are keeping the church from experiencing God's blessings, and refuse to allow the shepherd to lead the flock, there will be no impetus for renewal.

When a church is more interested in self-conservation, it develops a barrier towards the community it is called to serve, which declares our needs are more important than your needs. Many a church is not interested in serving the community until it is in trouble and then it is done for survival reasons. People see through this approach and feel cheapened.

Final Church Revitalization Restart Observations

The desire to see the church grow once again is not the main reason churches seek assistance in church renewal! The main reason is that they fear the church is dying, near death, or the members have waited too long to do something about it. A reduction in the church's ability to offer ministries usually prompts its desire for a church revitalization restart. The desire to avoid the deathblow of a church compels many congregations to consider church revitalization efforts. Yet, most laity find it hard to allow someone to assist them and for fear they will reveal the very things that caused their decline.

Living with Your Head in the Sand

Restart church revitalizers seek to lead you to remove your head from the sands of confusion and avoidance. When you are unwilling to face current realities:

- **The challenges and difficulties you face will only get worse.** All of us have challenges in our churches certainly. Yet keeping our head in the sand only causes the situation to become more difficult and harder to tackle.
- **Your children's children are forsaken by the church.** I ask people all the time in declining churches if they love their grandchildren enough to make the necessary changes required to restart their church. The response I often get has more to do with their own interests and their own wants and little to do with reaching future generations for Christ.
- **Most pastors have regrets about serving a group of individuals who opt out of making a difference for Christ.** Pastors want to reach people and change the world. They want the church to be relevant and as current as today's newspaper. Pastoral regrets surface often as a result of an unwillingness of the laity to want

to do something highly significant for the Kingdom of God. When laity hide their heads in the sand it only furthers problematic situations, not eliminates them.

- **Your membership becomes unwilling to work together as a team to restart your church.** Failure to focus the congregation together often brings a lack of connection and camaraderie to the task of restarting a church. Facing reality is the starting place.

- **Urgency is eliminated and there becomes a failure to launch and begin the effort to restart.** Change is all around us and yet the local church often struggles with change. We live in a day where the speed of change is accelerated and yet many churches decline to keep up. They are then shocked to realize in a few years just how irrelevant they have become.

- **You focus on the same old things with very little to show for it.** Such a maintenance mentality only fosters ongoing conflict and struggle. Keeping the status quo only hurts the church's ability to attract others. Your progressive church leaders become frustrated and eventually give up on you as the pastor leader and the church as a whole. When you have nowhere to go all that is left is the ability for people to blame each other and no one do anything about it.

- **Disobedience becomes the norm.** Living in a mode of denial nurtures a lack of willingness to serve as a witness to the world.

- **Mediocrity is allowed.** An emphasis on not making waves or rocking the boat causes churches that need to be restarted to stomach flagrant sin for the good of the status quo. When sin is allowed to be accepted and even left unconfronted, the church is on a spiral decline that is meteoric at best.

- **The best and the most committed will take flight.** Strong church members who are committed more to the Lord over an institution will leave once they sense that no one is going to address the real issues requiring a restart. The very members that your church needs in order to restart it often sense that the church does not want to make such a turn and off they go to a more committed church telling them how unwilling you are to follow scripture.

- **You have become comfortable with being comfortable.** So many churches get into a rut of contentment. The ability to make the changes necessary for revitalization becomes a blur due to a lack of focus on becoming a healthy New Testament church once more. Entrenched laity unwilling to do anything more than show up hurts the chances for a restart.

When you are unwilling to face current realities and live instead in a cocoon of denial, not seeking to handle surfacing problems, you are faced with a clear reality that you might be closing your doors to never open them again. That was not what Christ had in mind, nor the people who sacrificed greatly to plant your church originally.

Restarting a church is a journey of hope for a local struggling church that is facing hard decisions. In light of its future, decisions must be made regarding what it will do to ensure a Gospel lighthouse remains in the community where it was placed for many more years until Jesus comes to take all of us to Glory. Take the journey with those in your area that are working to revitalize churches for the sake of Christ. Become willing to embrace the opportunity for your church to survive rather than close down in failure. Allow the Lord God to bring forth a miracle for your church as He transforms the work of ministry within your midst. Restarting churches is a long distance relay run by marathoners not sprinters. You must be willing to invest a minimum of 1000 days into church renewal. Anything less, do not get involved. Pray that the Lord will rise up a group of committed new leaders with the energy to work and turn your church around. Ask God to bring new families into your worship center that have never heard the gospel message and are now drawn to hear the glorious message of salvation in Christ Jesus. Seek transformation not stagnation. Ask the Lord to transform your church, each one of you as individual worshippers and Christ followers. Watch how God will transform your individual families and bring a new expression of "church" right where you live.

The desire to see the church grow once again is not the main reason churches seek assistance in church restarting! The main reason is that they fear the church is dying, near death, or the members have waited too long to do something about it! A reduction in the church's ability to offer ministries usually prompts its desire for a church revitalization restart. The desire to avoid the deathblow of a church compels many congregations to consider church revitalization efforts! Yet, most laity find it hard to allow someone to assist them and reveal the very things that caused their decline.

Conclusion

Changing the mindset of the residual membership can often be very difficult. Senior adults occupy most of these candidate restart churches for which change is often hard to come by. Until the church is ready to make drastic changes, it is useless to become involved. There are thousands of churches like this all over America: Some are Baptists, others are Methodists, even in the Assemblies you can find them, Presbyterians, the Lutherans have them, Congregational, Christian, and many others, waiting for a mission-minded congregation to get involved in offering "new life."

One startling phenomenon is that there are churches today that as the laity begin to depart this life often see nothing wrong with taking the church to the grave as well. That was never part of God's plan for the very thing He gave up His life.

When a local church refuses to trade its fear of closing the door for a desire to see life come back within the congregation, the church revitalization experience will end promptly as soon as the danger of death has been eliminated. What happens next may mean another recycle of decline until it is bad again. Churches only experience renewal when their people experience renewal! Unless a church's leadership wants renewal, it will not happen. There must be a commitment to lead the church towards revitalization. If not, nothing will be changed. Church renewal must shift from a few being interested to eventually a full effort of the entire congregation. Revitalization is not a secret journey but a public one.

When a church is more interested in self-conservation, it develops a barrier towards the community it is called to serve, which declares our needs are more important than your needs. Many a church is not interested in serving its community until it is in trouble itself and then it is done for survival reasons. People will see right through this approach and feel cheapened.

The challenge of a church revitalization leader is not to impart renewal ability into your people, but to extract it, for the capacity is already there. Pastor, if your church is in downward spiral of plateau and decline, check some of these indicators out. In western Christianity, there is an emerging trend that is alarming to say the least if not unscriptural. Some congregations have decided or are deciding right now that it is easier to die rather than live. Too many churches are attended and led mostly by people who are quite happy for their church to plateau and decline. They recognize that they are personally getting older and will eventually die, and their expectation is that their church will decline with them and also eventually die. They have no vision for the church being revitalized and are not willing to make any of the changes that might be necessary for this to happen. Indeed, they resist change of any kind. They welcome new members, including younger ones, but only if these people conform to the way things have always been done.

There is an ever-growing problem with declining attendance and membership in the church today! Once a church begins to become stuck it must work hard at overcoming such a crippling obstacle. There are a whole host of problems and issues when it comes to tackling "stuckness" within a church that eventually leads to decline.

Because churches can be elderly heavy, or elderly members hold the positions of control, it becomes extremely complicated to make changes. This is especially so as the benefits of doing so are often a long time in coming.

Dealing with stuckness means a lot of work, and there are often few people who have both the time and the leaning to take on all the extra work. This means that burnout can happen rapidly, and initiatives fail as the two or three people become dispirited that their efforts seem to be producing less than acceptable results.

Often a church's inability to adapt to the changing cultural mix within its ministry area will lead to eventual stuckness. Our world is changing and any church that refuses to change along with it will one day find itself struggling to overcome the sense of decline, plateau and the feeling of being stuck!

It is impossible to keep everyone happy. There is often a huge difference in worshipping styles of the old and the young. Maintaining a "something for everyone" style can sometimes work, or certainly seem to work initially, but as one or other group tends to be larger, this practice can often slip, or those that were willing to put up with it previously, vote with their feet and go where their needs and interests can be met.

If a stuck church finds itself in a socially and economically deprived area, people tend to take much longer to change their mindsets. This means that a church must provide them with something they need or like. This could include some form of community, friendships, advice, or support systems. If the church cannot give them something to hold their interest, or address a felt need, they usually will drift.

Many stuck churches are unable to fight off the disease feeling of stuckness. They are unable to delay the decay that is fast approaching. The sense of diminished impact and continual deterioration stalls the church and a feeling of being stuck begins to drift in and cause the church to become less of an impact.

Most of these stuck churches don't have the luxury of a full time minister anymore; this removes the figurehead from the church, the central role of authority. Changing the way a whole army of lay volunteers (who do a fantastic job) do things is almost impossible, so there is often no consistency in a church service from week to week.

Financially, most stuck churches are not doing so well. Some have reserves, but live in fear of eating into them as this would then make them financially unsound. Couple this with low attendance and we are talking church closure.

Is there any hope for a stuck church in this condition? Well, nothing is impossible with God, and he could revive such a church with his Holy Spirit.

Some things that work usually and have worked in the past are: a new younger pastor with a strong vision; a laity who senses one last chance for growth and victory as there is a stirring up of any remaining embers of true spiritual life.

Change is slow and if you are always the first out of the starting gate you will become very frustrated because there will be times where you feel you are beating a dead horse to keep it running! God can restore your church once again! But if you are too hardheaded and hard hearted to change yourself, then you are probably not able to bring about repair, refocus, renewal, and revitalization. God wants to change His church and He desires to use you and me. Isn't that amazing? Our humble dependence coupled with a forward looking faith might just be all that it will take for God to use you as a renewal participant. You and your church can either be a brief scene from the TV show *Desperate Housewives* or you can watch God lead you forward into greater victory than you have seen in some time. The choice is yours.

Pastor, just as assuredly you will at times in your ministry when you discover that you have outgrown your people within the congregation; there will also be times where they have outgrown you. When this happens it might be time to re-dream what God wants for this church. Sometimes He will use stuckness to show all of you the way. Watch out for the drift and be cautious with disassociating oneself from the whole membership. Say engaged while running with the runners. Remember that as a leader any miss-steps will not only hurt you but it can also paralyze a congregation so steady goes it at the helm. As you grow in this area of church revitalization you will see yourself taking ownership and responsibility of key transformation projects and making solid renewal decisions. You will also look over your shoulder and discover to your great amazement, that there is still a large contingent of the faithful following joyfully behind you desiring all the time that you lead them out of this predicament and into a greater if not the greatest day for the Lord and His work as you call on the family of faith right where you live.

The Church must begin to address some key issues for revitalization:

- The need for new initiatives (new avenues).

- The need for new entrance points into the church.

- The updating of present ministries and programs.

- How the church will care for its new and present participants.

- The long-term development of disciples.

- The present and future staff equipping.

- How the laity will be matured in the faith and enlisted in the work of the ministry.

- The examination of any areas of work that are becoming dead weight to renewal efforts.

- How to let go of ministries that are no longer serving the church.

- Remember groups leading ministries that are left on their own will usually justify the plans that long-time members have invested in regardless of their outcome for growth.

A recent study revealed an astonishing fact. A study has revealed that there are churches that are 190 to 200 years old that are thriving. They are culturally relevant and lasting relationships are being built each and every day.[100] No church is beyond the power of God to transform it. Remember it is God's timetable and not yours, it will take some time so be patient. Display a courageous faith daily in the midst of the transformation. Get up and go to work each day allowing the Lord to guide your hands. Though it is daunting and often risky, the uncharted paths will move all of us out of those comfortable places into the unsure places where God can stretch us, expand us, grow us and in the end revitalize us once again into a healthy revitalized church. Pray! Pray some more. Now pray even a little more! Lastly, be reassured that the Lord on high will use your church to His glory once again. Remember to give God the praise when He does.

Wrapping it up!

A key factor in congregational decline is the failure to introduce new members to disciple making and equip them in the disciple-making mission of the church. Observe a few key paths for the local church seeking revitalization and renewal:

---

[100] Olson, pg.136.

- Place a larger emphasis on Disciple making!

- Show your faith in and to your community (Acts 2:42)!

- Share your life within the community (2 Cor. 8:3-5)!

- Remember the church is people and they are the key to renewal (1 Thess. 2:8)!

- Equip others for the harvest field!

- Develop new leaders for leadership!

- Move past self-preservation to self-sacrifice for the cause of Christ!

- Avoid copying others' renewal efforts and begin listening, discerning, and responding to the Lord's leading!

- Develop ways for the laity to give themselves to others!

- Help the church to face the current realities of its ministry. Truth is not an enemy of the new!

- Discover what has changed around your ministry area during the last 20 years. Most churches do not know!

- Help your people dream a little about what could be!

- Do not wait too long to begin to revitalize your church!

- Understand that there is a huge cost involved

in church revitalization and it will take a combined effort of laity and ministers to see renewal come to fruition!

You must have a "begin the journey" point in time with church revitalization. It is easier to go to meetings and talk about church revitalization than to begin working in church revitalization. If you are not careful the task force can spend more time talking about what "we are going to do" than getting to doing it.

ABOUT THE AUTHOR
Dr. Tom Cheyney
Founder & Directional Leader
Renovate National Church Revitalization Conference
RenovateConference.org
ChurchRevitalizer.guru
tom@renovateconference.org

Tom is the founder and directional leader of the RENOVATE National Church Revitalization Conference, Executive Editor of the *Church Revitalizer Magazine*, and leader of the RENOVATE Church Revitalization Virtual Coaching Network where he mentors pastors, churches, and denominational leaders in Church Revitalization and Renewal all across North America. He serves as the National Host of the weekly *Church Revitalization and Renewal Podcast*. Dr. Cheyney has written over 5,000 print, audio resources, guides, or books for church revitalizers, pastors, church planters, and lay leaders. His most recent books include: *The Nuts and Bolts of Church Revitalization (along with Terry Tials)*; *Thirty-Eight Church Revitalization Models for the Twenty First Century* and *Preaching Towards Church Revitalization and Renewal (along with Larry Wynn)*. Cheyney has written along, with his friend Rodney Harrison, *Spin-Off Churches* (B&H Publishers). Tom is a nationally recognized conference speaker and a frequent writer on church revitalization, church planting, new church health, and leadership development. Others have labeled Tom as the **Father of the Church Revitalization Movement**, as his influence has stretched across multiple denominations and countries.

Other Books by Tom Cheyney

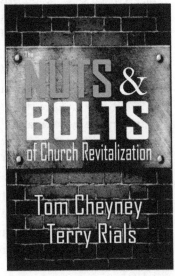

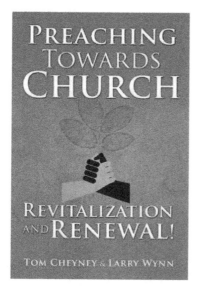

Made in United States
Orlando, FL
11 July 2022

19655267R00065